Finding Comfort
in God's Embrace

Finding Comfort in God's Embrace

31 Meditations for Those Who Grieve

Gwen Waller

Foreword by David Waller, Ph.D.
Illustrations by Kim Bergland

MAIN STREET BOOK HOUSE
AUBURN, WASHINGTON

MAIN STREET BOOK HOUSE
Auburn, Washington
Finding Comfort in God's Embrace
Copyright © 2005 by Gwendolyn M. Waller
Cover photo © Benjamin Cross
Interior graphics by Kim Bergland
Design and layout by Leslie Sierra (www.LeslieSierra.com)
Published by Main Street Book House

Printed in the United States of America

Finding Comfort in God's Embrace may be ordered through bookstores or directly from Main Street Book House. Quantity discounts are available. To order or for more information, contact us at www.mainstreetbookhouse.com or write to:
Main Street Book House
P.O. Box 607
Auburn, WA 98071-0607

ISBN 0-9740737-0-9
Library of Congress Control Number: 2005933010

DEDICATION

*To Darren and Dad, who have reached
heaven's shores, and to my family and friends
who continue to journey with me.*

Contents

Part One

Finding Comfort in God's Nearness

Part Two

Finding Comfort in God's Compassion

Part Three

Finding Comfort in God's Strength

PART EIGHT

Finding Comfort in God's Love

ACKNOWLEDGMENTS

I never can adequately thank our family and friends who walked with us down the road of grief. You were God's arms of comfort.

I also am grateful to those who have entrusted to me their pain and have allowed me to share their stories with others. Thank you for joining with me in striving to comfort others with "the comfort we ourselves have received from God" (2 Corinthians 1:4).

I could not have completed this book without the support of my dear friends and prayer partners. You spurred me on when I was tempted to give up.

Bev Miller at Main Street Book House, you also helped me persevere and provided valuable expertise. Kim Bergland and Leslie Sierra, your vision and artistic abilities have been a tremendous blessing.

Brent and Scott, it broke my heart to see your pain in losing your baby brother. But your faith in God and His goodness encouraged us all. And Daniel, though you never met Darren, your faith has inspired us as well. I love and appreciate you all.

Finally, David, thank you for walking this road with me. Thank you, too, for believing in this book and for enriching it with your wisdom and expertise. I love you and appreciate your partnership, in times of joy and times of sorrow.

Foreword

As a clinical psychologist and pastor, I have sat with many who were grieving losses. The death of my son Darren enlarged my heart for those who are mourning.

Grief is like the waves of the sea. As a teenager, I bodysurfed and will never forget the power of the ocean. One moment I would be riding a wave, deceived into thinking I had mastered it. Suddenly it gripped me and threw me to the ocean floor, where I lay pinned. I thought my lungs would burst and I would drown, unable to overcome the awesome power of the water that had fallen on me. Then, suddenly, I was released as the wave rolled by. Pressing against the ocean floor, I would shoot myself up to the surface, gasping for air, happy to breathe again. Other times I would not be pinned, but instead be tossed and twisted until I had no sense of which way was up and which was down. I learned not to panic. The wave would pass, and I would feel the ocean floor or float to the surface and find my way to a life-giving breath.

I experienced grief much like these waves. One moment I was doing OK, mastering my life again; the next, I was struggling for air, feeling overcome by grief. Then the wave would pass, but I knew that more waves eventually would come. I learned, as in surfing, to not fight that which was more powerful than me. I learned to not fear or panic in its grip, but instead to trust that I would find my way to the surface again.

The purpose of grief is to protect our souls. God designed it to sustain us in times of great loss. It can insulate us and slow us down. Grief is a productive depression, which works the loss through our soul. In some ways it is like a clinical depression, as we may experience some or all of the same symptoms: a depressed mood of sadness, disturbance of our appetite and/or sleep, loss of motivation and purpose, reduced ability to concentrate, difficulty with memory, loss of pleasure with life, wanting to withdraw from others, thoughts of hopelessness or wishing we could die, and a lowered self-esteem. Grief and clinical depression are different, however, because grief is a productive depression, moving us through the loss. Clinical depression is unproductive, as we stay stuck in the loss. No progress is made.

As a clinical psychologist, I help people in depression get unstuck and begin productively mourning their losses, present or past. As a grieving father, I needed to work through it myself, and it was frightening. My hands went numb, symbolizing my sense of helplessness in not being able to protect or hold my son and of having him wrenched from my strong grip. I felt sad, cried, lost my appetite, and sighed a lot, as if I could not get enough air (those waves again). I had trouble concentrating and remembering. I also lost energy and seemed to run at half speed, yet I could not sleep. I wondered, would it end? Would life be "normal" again?

Watching my wife, Gwen, grieve was even more frightening. I had a sense that I would somehow survive the grief, but would she? Or would she get stuck in her mourning? I again sensed my helplessness. So I followed the wisdom I offer to my depressed clients, "Learn to take back your power." I decided to control that which was in my control and release myself and my wife to the waves of grief, trusting God that we would surface in time for air.

I trusted God to use this productive depression, this mourning, to protect and move my soul to a new place. I trusted Him to do the same for my wife. I promised God and myself that I would experience my grief to its fullest. I would give myself time to experience every feeling. This was more difficult to do than I imagined. I had to work and care for my family, so I could not fully experience my grief throughout each day. I had to contain it for periods of time, so I could function, and then release it. Sometimes I was so good at holding back the grief that, late at night, I needed to actively provoke it. I would read a book about loss or listen to music. Then a wave of grief would come and overwhelm me. I would sob in the silent hours of the night while my wife, children, and clients slept. At times I also shared my experience, thoughts, and feelings with my wife and my closest friends. I needed them to be mirrors and to understand me, and they did not let me down. They allowed me to grieve. This permission to mourn freed me to move through a productive depression. The darkness began to pass.

My wife has written this book to help you, too, grieve productively. She has written brief meditations, knowing that mourning impairs one's ability to concentrate for long periods. You may need to read each one two or three times, to let them sink into your soul. She also has written this book so you do not feel so alone. She wants to give you hope, knowing that the waves are real and powerful, but they will pass. You will breathe again.

Within this book, you will read about the hope our family found in our God and Savior, Jesus. Gwen invites you to find Him more clearly in your mourning, and to find people who will journey with you, whether friends, family, or professionals.

God's grace to you in your journey. I pray that you will allow Him to see you through. May your grief be productive in insulating your soul and enlarging your heart. May His face shine upon you, and may you comfort those who grieve after you with the same comfort He nurtured in you.

David Waller, Ph.D.
Licensed Psychologist
Pastor of Adults, Grace Community Church
Auburn, Washington

INTRODUCTION

On September 23, 1993, I gave birth to our third son, Darren Jonathan Waller. My husband, David, and I had anticipated holding him closely moments after his arrival, as we had our first two sons. Instead, we watched a medical team feverishly work to revive him. Then, rather than putting Darren in my arms, they put him in an incubator, connected him to life support, and flew him to another hospital. The doctors strongly suspected that our baby had trisomy 18, a chromosomal abnormality that, in their words, "is not compatible with life."

For four days, David and I held Darren as much as the tubes and wires would allow. Our other sons, seven-year-old Brent and four-year-old Scott, also scrubbed and donned sterile gowns so that they could hold their brother. Many joined us in hoping and praying for a miracle. Meanwhile, the monitors showed that our son's heart and lungs were failing.

On the fourth day, blood tests confirmed the diagnosis of trisomy 18. Doctors explained that if we continued medical intervention, we would be prolonging Darren's death, not his life. After praying and seeking wise counsel, we agreed to his removal from life support. Then David, Brent, Scott, and I held and loved Darren for the brief moments before he entered Jesus' arms.

That night we left the hospital brokenhearted. We never had known such pain and grief. But we also never had known such comfort as that which God provided in the following weeks, months, and years. We always will love and miss Darren, but eventually God mended our broken hearts. He also graciously gave us a fourth son, Daniel, to love and to raise.

In time, God even enabled us to share His comfort with

others, which is why I have written this book. It was not my idea; it was my friend Laura's, whose sixteen-year-old daughter had been murdered. One night, at the end of a grief support group I was leading, Laura turned to me and said, "You should write a devotional book for people who are grieving."

I immediately declined her challenge. In the coming months, however, God led me to begin this collection of meditations. I admit that it has not been easy. In relaying others' stories and our own experience, I have relived some of our pain. But I also have remembered God's grace and faithfulness. I have continued to find comfort in Him.

I pray that as you read this book you, too, will find encouragement from others who have gone before you and from the Lord, who longs to go with you. I suggest that you read one meditation each day your first time through. Later you may find it helpful to review specific sections as needed. Each meditation concludes with a prayer and "Embracing God's Comfort." As you feel comfortable, I invite you to use these suggested applications to help you work through your grief. Space is provided to write your responses to the applications and to journal other thoughts and feelings.

May you find healing in these pages and comfort in God's embrace.

PART ONE

Finding Comfort
in
God's Nearness

*"God is our refuge and strength, an
ever-present help in trouble."*
~ Psalm 46:1 ~

Closer Than Our Tears

"The Lord is close to the brokenhearted and saves those who are crushed in spirit." ~ Psalm 34:18

My body trembled as I rose from my hospital bed and made my way down the hall to the neonatal unit. How could I even try to sleep? My arms ached for my newborn son. If the doctor's initial diagnosis were correct, this night would be one of my only opportunities to hold Darren.

When I reached the sterile unit, a nurse quickly helped me into a chair. She gently handed me my baby, carefully maneuvering the tubes and wires that sustained his life. As I cradled him in my arms, I heard the monitor register his feeble heartbeat. What could keep his heart from failing, and mine from breaking?

Never before had I suffered such anguish, so never before had I noticed Psalm 34:18. Then, while Darren lingered between life and death, I read it on a note from a friend. I reread it, I embraced it, I clung to it. This promise became my comfort and my refuge, just as it had been for Diane, who inscribed it on the card. She, too, was brokenhearted, having recently buried her stillborn daughter.

The original author, David, was no stranger to trials and grief. He wrote Psalm 34 soon after King Saul tried to kill him. In later years, he mourned the death of three sons and his dear friend Jonathan. Throughout these and other hardships, the psalmist called out to the Lord and found peace in His presence.

After my son's death I, too, cried out to God for understanding and comfort. I vividly remember one night when I fell to my knees beside our bed and poured out my broken heart in prayer. Why had He, the sovereign Lord, allowed this excruciating pain in my life? I was especially confused because, before conceiving Darren, I finally had released my dream of a larger family and felt content with our two children. Then God had given us a third, only to take him away after four short days. Didn't He care, or was I just a pawn in His celestial chess game?

That night I held nothing back. Then, drained of tears and anger, I fell face down on the floor and waited for the lightening bolt to strike. After all, who was I to be enraged with the holy God of the universe? Instead of being struck down, however, I sensed God's loving acceptance and comforting embrace. My eyes again welled with tears, but this time they flowed from a heart of thanksgiving for His tender mercy.

Just as no two persons' losses are identical, neither are their encounters with God. Even my own experience varied from day to day. At times I knew God's nearness through caring individuals He sent our way. Friends, family, and fellow believers—Christ's body here on earth—reached out to help meet our emotional and physical needs. God also made His presence known through His Word, where I found comfort, guidance, hope, and His expressions of love. And sometimes I sensed His indwelling Spirit comforting me and carrying me through my day.

On other days, I questioned God's nearness. He seemed distant, aloof. I wrestled with doubts, then chose to remember that His Word is true; I need not feel His presence to know that He is with me. God is indeed "close to the brokenhearted and saves those who are crushed in spirit."

As you draw near to Him and pour out your broken heart, may He embrace you with His everlasting, ever-loving arms. He sees your tears and truly longs to be near you during this time of grief…and forever.

Heavenly Father, thank You for Your nearness in my time of pain. May I experience Your presence and comfort today as You hold me close in Your loving arms. Even when You seem far away, may I know that You are closer than my tears. Amen.

Embracing God's Comfort

I invite you to read Psalm 34 and write down what the psalmist says about God. From this passage of Scripture, what encourages you most?

_____

_____

_____

_____

_____

_____

_____

_____

_____

_____

_____

Finding Comfort
in Our Shepherd's Care

"The Lord is my shepherd, I shall not be in want.
He makes me lie down in green pastures,
he leads me beside quiet waters,
he restores my soul.
He guides me in paths of righteousness for his name's sake.
Even though I walk through the valley
of the shadow of death,
I will fear no evil,
for you are with me;
your rod and your staff, they comfort me."
~ Psalm 23:1-4 ~

Four months after we had buried our infant son, I turned to Psalm 23 for comfort. Instead I found incongruity. David wrote, "I shall not be in want," but how else could I define the emptiness in my heart? I desperately wanted Darren back. My love for my child had not disappeared, but now I had no way of expressing it to him. How my arms ached to hold him.

Before I could read further in the Scripture, I needed to cry out to God, to voice my frustration and longing. Why had I been robbed of the opportunity to know my son and to see him grow up? I had anticipated teaching him, playing with him, delighting in him, and loving him. Unlike the psalmist, I was not content. Although the Lord was my shepherd, I felt "in want."

Then, as I meditated on Psalm 23, the Lord gently reminded me that I may want more in this life, but I never am lacking, because I have Him. The God of the universe loves me and has chosen me to be His. In His strength, He protects me; with His wisdom, He guides me. When I experience difficulties in this world, "He restores my soul." Even in the dismal and terrifying "valley of the shadow of death," His presence comforts me.

I recognized anew that true contentment cannot be found in the things of this world—not even in loving relationships. God did not condemn me for wishing that Darren could be restored to me, to love and to raise, but He reminded me that my son was not the answer to my longings. In my loving, ever-present Shepherd, I truly do have everything I need.

Does this mean we will stop missing those who have left this world? No, our love for our children, spouses, parents, and other special people in our lives does not die with them. Nor does this promise answer our questions of why we have had to pass through this dismal valley of grief.

We can find comfort, however, in the tender care and continual presence of our Savior. He loved us so much that He laid down His own life that we might join His flock and enjoy an eternal relationship with Him. As Jesus said, "I am the good shepherd; I know my sheep and my sheep know me....I give them eternal life, and they shall never perish; no one can snatch them out of my hand" (John 10:14, 28).

How reassuring to know that, whether our paths lead through grassy meadows or dark valleys, we can feel safe, secure, and content knowing that our Good Shepherd walks beside us. Along the way He guides and nurtures us, meeting our needs and demonstrating His devotion. Someday He will lead us home to enjoy His presence for all eternity. Thus we can join the psalmist in saying, "The Lord is my shepherd, I shall not be in want."

Loving Shepherd, thank You for protecting, providing, leading, and comforting me. You know how much I love and miss the one I have lost. Help me to know how much You love and cherish me, Your precious sheep. May I find contentment in my intimate and eternal relationship with You. Amen.

Embracing God's Comfort

Read through Psalm 23, noting what God, your shepherd, will do for you. Focus on one of these actions and consider what it means to you right now. Thank God for this aspect of His role as your shepherd, and ask Him to help you depend on Him to care for you.

_____

_____

_____

_____

_____

_____

_____

_____

_____

_____

Secure in His Hands

"The steps of a man are established by the Lord;
and He delights in his way. When he falls, he shall
not be hurled headlong; because the Lord is the One
who holds his hand." ~ Psalm 37:23-24 (NASB)

As our family hiked in the mountains one summer, we encountered a glazed snowfield across our path. My husband's and my boots provided adequate traction, but our four-year-old son's well-worn shoes did not. As I peered down the long, steep, slippery slope, I was grateful that, despite his independent spirit, Daniel willingly clung to his dad's hand as they crossed. Each time our son started to slide, David held him secure, ensuring his safe arrival on the other side.

The psalmist David knew that everyone crosses treacherous paths during their journeys on earth. Even those who closely follow God, as the psalmist did, experience grueling trials. They also experience God's abiding presence in the midst of their difficulties. He assures us that "the Lord upholds the righteous....and will not forsake his faithful ones....The Lord helps them and delivers them" (Psalm 37:17, 28, 40).

I am thankful for God's nearness and care throughout my life. In high school I first realized He was reaching down, inviting me to receive His love and forgiveness and to take His hand. I eagerly accepted. Though I often have let Him down, He never has let go. As a college student, I foolishly tried to squirm free from my heavenly Father to follow my misguided peers. Even then He graciously clung to my hand and drew me back to His side, not allowing me to be "hurled headlong."

More recently, as I stumbled in anger and confusion over my son's death, my faithful Father stayed with me. When I expressed my rage and doubted His devotion, He continued to lovingly hold my hand, walking me through the steps laid out before me. Though death had cast a frightening shadow across my path, God's presence gave me courage to keep moving ahead, trusting Him for the unknown. His light even enabled me to see some of the beauty and goodness along the way.

For each of us, God has blazed a trail through our grief, and He longs to hold our hands as we journey together. As the psalmist clearly depicts, He does not yank us along gruffly, like an exasperated father dragging his whimpering child. Rather, He delights in us as we depend upon Him. As we tremble with fear, His strong hand calms us and securely leads us. Each time we trip and stumble, He holds us tightly yet tenderly, protecting us from serious harm. And when our eyes are so filled with tears that we cannot even see the path under our feet, His gentle hand soothes us and guides us.

May we find comfort in this precious snapshot of our God. The One who created everything and holds it all together also desires to hold us. We need only place our hand in His. Then we can face each day, assured that He walks beside us and never will let us go until He has ushered us home to dwell in His glorious presence forever.

Father, thank You for reaching down in love and inviting me to take Your hand. I am grateful that You keep me from being "hurled headlong" when I stumble over life's difficulties and tragedies. Help me to always trust in Your presence and to cling tightly to Your loving hand. Amen.

Embracing God's Comfort

What will help you cling to your loving Father's outstretched hand today? Perhaps you hesitate to even reach up because you're not sure that you are His child. God's Word promises, "To all who received him [Jesus], to those who believed in his name, he gave the right to become children of God" (John 1:12). To be adopted by the heavenly Father, you need only admit your need and accept the gift of Jesus' death on the cross for your sins. Then reach up and take hold of your loving Father's outstretched hand. He cares about you and longs to help you.

_____

_____

_____

_____

_____

_____

_____

_____

God Never Says Good-Bye

*"Be strong and courageous. Do not be afraid or
terrified...for the Lord your God goes with you; he
will never leave you nor forsake you....The Lord
himself goes before you and will be with you; he will
never leave you nor forsake you. Do not be afraid;
do not be discouraged." ~ Deuteronomy 31:6, 8*

"Do not be discouraged"? How could Jo Ann feel anything
else? The two years since her husband's death had been filled
with emotional and financial hardship. Raising two teenagers
was challenging, and she longed for their father's wisdom
and support. At times she felt so alone, and her heart ached
for the man she loved so deeply.

Yet Jo Ann knew that she was not alone. So when she began
to despair, she called out to the One who loves her most
and never can be torn away from her. For three days, in the
solitude of a beach cabin, Jo Ann prayed everything that was
on her grieving heart. In her Bible, she found God's loving
and specific answers. She returned home strengthened by
His powerful and personal presence.

Moses, too, had experienced God's mighty presence, so as
he approached his death, he confidently told the Israelites,
"Don't be afraid...God goes with you." But it was much easier
for him to say than for them to live. The Israelites would
have to finish their journey to the Promised Land without
their leader.

Moses spoke to their concern by reminding them that,
while he was leaving them, God never would. They need
not fear the future or the enemies they would encounter, for
God would be with them and go before them. Throughout
Moses' final words he encouraged them with the promise of

God's constant presence.

As soon as Moses died, his replacement, Joshua, needed to again be reminded of God's nearness. Stepping into Moses' sandals would be especially difficult at this time, as Joshua grieved the loss of his close friend and trusted leader. Yet God instructed him, "Moses my servant is dead. Now then, you and all these people, get ready to cross the Jordan River into the land I am about to give to them—to the Israelites" (Joshua 1:2).

God would give them the land, but not gift-wrapped. Joshua and his troops would need to march forth in faith to conquer what the Lord had promised them. Yet Joshua is told not to feel threatened by those who try to stand in the way. Such enemies would come and go, but his Lord never would leave his side. God repeatedly admonished him to be strong and courageous because, "As I was with Moses, so I will be with you; I will never leave you nor forsake you" (Joshua 1:5).

More than 1,000 years later, God encouraged another group of people with the same promise. The writer of Hebrews assured persecuted Jewish Christians that, no matter what anyone in the world took from them, they could find satisfaction and courage in their relationship with God. "Be content with what you have, because God has said, 'Never will I leave you; never will I forsake you.' So we say with confidence, 'The Lord is my helper; I will not be afraid. What can man do to me?'" (Hebrews 13:5-6).

We, too, may fear or dread our future in the absence of our loved ones. God does not criticize us, but compassionately offers the comfort and hope of His loving presence. If Christ is our Savior, then His Spirit has taken up permanent residence within us. He who knows everything we will face today, tomorrow, next month, and next year goes before us and walks with us each moment of each day.

The death of a loved one often means not only intense

anguish, but also added responsibilities, as Joshua and my friend Jo Ann faced. How can we carry such duties when we already are weighted down with grief? Strength and courage are found in knowing we need not bear such burdens alone. "The Lord is my helper," the writer of Hebrews assures us.

God may manifest His help and presence in people around us. While I generally resist letting others serve me, when my son died I surrendered and said "yes" when friends offered to vacuum, iron, and cook for us. Bearing my sorrow sapped my strength for even these routine tasks.

Do you need help carrying additional financial, legal, parenting, and personal responsibilities? God may meet some of these needs through the people around you. He also invites you to spend time in prayer and His Word, drawing strength and hope from His presence, as Jo Ann did.

Remember, just as He was with Moses, Joshua, the Israelites, and the persecuted Hebrew Christians, God is with you. Never will He forsake you; never will He fail you. You can depend on Him.

Lord, what comfort I find in Your constant presence. Thank You that, while those I love here on earth may leave me, You never will leave me or let me down. May I look to You continually as my strength and comfort for each day. Amen.

Embracing God's Comfort

What do you fear most as you face the future without your loved one? How might God's presence help you deal with this fear?

_____

_____

_____

_____

_____

_____

_____

_____

_____

_____

_____

_____

PART TWO

Finding Comfort
in
God's Compassion

"The Lord is full of compassion and mercy."
~ James 5:11 ~

Time to Praise God?

"Praise be to the God and Father of our Lord Jesus Christ, the Father of compassion and the God of all comfort, who comforts us in all our troubles, so that we can comfort those in any trouble with the comfort we ourselves have received from God." ~ 2 Corinthians 1:3-4

I marched over and turned off the stereo. I was not in the mood for joyful singers telling me it was time to praise God. It was not time! At least not by my clock. I still was too ticked to talk of God's goodness. Nor could I bring myself to exalt the Lord's sovereignty and power, as in so doing I would acknowledge He could have kept our son alive, but did not. Only after I worked through my anger and confusion and I surrendered my will could I give God the uncensored praise He always deserves.

Yet, even in those early days of my grief, I could offer heartfelt praise for God's constant presence and sustaining strength. I also appreciated His bountiful grace and love. And I could readily join the apostle Paul in exalting the Lord for His comfort and compassion, which I experienced as His loving arms carried me through the darkest hours of my grief.

We may wonder why God allows our suffering, but we need never question if He understands our pain. As the "Father of our Lord Jesus Christ," He sympathizes with us, having experienced the excruciating separation of death when His only Son hung on the cross. These verses also assure us that He cares. "The Father of compassion and the God of all comfort...comforts us in all our troubles." As parents reach out to soothe their children when they run home with scraped knees or wounded hearts, our heavenly Father longs to console us in our grief. He pours out His comfort and compassion; we need only open our arms and hearts to receive it.

Sometimes I experienced His comfort as I read His Word. Throughout the Psalms I saw His love and faithfulness, His mercy and strength. In the gospels I read that He is "the bread of life" (John 6:35), sustaining me, and "the light of the world" (John 9:5), casting out the darkness of my despair. At other times I sensed God's presence as I cried out to Him in prayer, sharing my heart and catching a glimpse of His. I also saw the Lord's compassion when others extended to us His loving arms. Whether it was a card, a hug, a meal, or cleaning my house the night before Darren's funeral, these actions communicated God's comfort.

As time has passed, God's comfort has proven sufficient not only for me but also for others who are in the midst of suffering. I identify more closely with their pain and am compelled to reach out in compassion. As Paul wrote in 2 Corinthians 1, having experienced God's comfort enables me to share it with those who hurt.

Looking back on the Lord's outpouring of compassion, first to me and then through me, prompts me to lift my voice in praise of His goodness, and even His sovereignty and power. Going through and growing through my grief has increased my appreciation for all of God's attributes. Now my heart sincerely and joyfully sings, yes, it is time to praise the Lord.

Lord, even when my anger blocks my praise from flowing freely, may I draw near to You as the "Father of compassion and the God of all comfort." Thank You for accepting me as You listen to my cries and for comforting me through Your Word and Your Body. I am grateful for those who have experienced Your compassion and expressed it to me. In time may I, too, be Your loving arms and share Your comfort with others. Amen.

Embracing God's Comfort

In 2 Corinthians 1:3,4, Paul writes that God comforts us in all our troubles. List your troubles and write down any ways that you have seen God comfort you. Thank Him for those expressions of love and call upon Him for His continuing compassion.

_____

_____

_____

_____

_____

_____

_____

_____

Finding Comfort in His Tears

"When Jesus saw her [Mary] weeping, and the Jews
who had come along with her also weeping, he was
deeply moved in spirit and troubled. 'Where have
you laid him?' he asked. 'Come and see, Lord,'
they replied. Jesus wept." ~ John 11:33-35

One evening, as our family sat around the dinner table, my husband invited everyone to share a Bible verse. Our eldest son, Brent, proudly recalled several verses he had memorized at camp. Then his brother Scott grinned and quickly recited an all-time favorite among children: "Jesus wept."

While Sunday school students are drawn to this verse by its brevity, in recent years I've been struck by its potency. "Jesus wept." The same Jesus who created all things and holds all things together, the One who not only knows the beginning and end but is the beginning and end, this same Jesus wept.

The story begins in John 11:1, where Jesus learned that His dear friend Lazarus was sick, yet He did not rush to heal him, as He had countless others. Instead, He waited two days, telling His disciples, "This sickness will not end in death. No, it is for God's glory so that God's Son may be glorified through it" (John 11:4).

Finally, knowing that Lazarus had died, Jesus went to his home in Bethany, where Lazarus' sisters and friends were mourning. Martha's first words to Jesus mirror the frustration many of us have expressed as we have asked, "Lord, you could have healed my loved one—why didn't You?" Jesus might have responded, "Who are you to question God?" but instead He lovingly assured her, "Your brother will rise again" (John 11:23).

Martha assumed Jesus was referring to the final resurrection of all believers; she had no idea Lazarus would be restored to life that very day. Yet, she reaffirmed her faith in her Lord and went to get her sister. Mary then ran to Jesus, fell at His feet, and cried out, "Lord, if you had been here, my brother would not have died" (John 11:32).

Again Jesus responded compassionately, neither accusing Mary of lacking faith nor defending His own actions. Then, seeing Mary and the others weeping, Jesus "was deeply moved in spirit and troubled" and began to cry. Even though He knew that in moments He would raise Lazarus from the grave, He grieved with His friends. And His eyes were not just a little moist—He sobbed. "Jesus wept."

Jesus' tears for His friend demonstrate His sympathy for us as well. He who created us for life knows that the separation of death causes excruciating pain for those left behind. Jesus Himself experienced that anguish when Lazarus lay in the grave and when His own death on the cross tore Him apart from His Father. Yet He submitted Himself to that agonizing separation, knowing that His death would enable us to be forever united with our God.

In our grief, may we draw strength from our Savior's sacrifice, through which He offers us a future and a hope. Jesus promised us, "I am the resurrection and the life. He who believes in me will live, even though he dies" (John 11:25). Jesus' victory over death assures us that all who trust in Him will be raised to eternal life.

May we also draw comfort from His compassion. He who already has experienced the joy of the resurrection also has experienced the sorrow of grief. He understands the tears we shed for those who have gone before us. Remember, "Jesus wept."

Jesus, I am so grateful that You are not an insensitive deity, but rather a caring, compassionate Friend. I find comfort in Your tears and hope in Your resurrection. Thank You, too, for Your gracious gift of eternal life, which strengthens me in the midst of my pain. I love You, Jesus. Amen.

Embracing God's Comfort

Close your eyes and picture Jesus standing or sitting before you. Express your frustration; ask Him questions. Then sit quietly, imagining Him weeping over the death of your loved one. When you feel ready, thank Him for weeping with you today, for deeply feeling with you the unnaturalness of death and the loss of a loved one.

_____

_____

_____

_____

_____

_____

_____

_____

_____

_____

Our Compassionate Father

"As a father has compassion on his children, so the Lord has compassion on those who fear him; for he knows how we are formed, he remembers that we are dust. As for man, his days are like grass, he flourishes like a flower of the field; the wind blows over it and it is gone, and its place remembers it no more. But from everlasting to everlasting the Lord's love is with those who fear him, and his righteousness with their children's children." ~ Psalm 103:13-17

In August 2005, Hurricane Katrina struck Mississippi and Louisiana, flooding homes and communities, separating loved ones, displacing residents, and taking lives. Across the United States, even those of us who were physically unaffected by the storm were brought to tears. Through television, newspapers, and the Internet, our minds were filled with vivid images of suffering and death; and our hearts were filled with sorrow.

We need no compassion for the prosperous, healthy, and happy, who walk with confidence and joy. Our sympathy is reserved for those who suffer; our pity, for those struck down by tragedy. When lives are taken through hurricanes, tsunamis, wars, cancer, car accidents, famines, senseless shooting sprees, and other tragedies, our hearts ache.

How much more our heavenly Father responds to the pain and grief of those who recognize their helplessness. God, in His strength, knows our frailty. He is mindful that we are like flowers of the field, at times basking in the sun, at times pounded by rain or hail and blown by winds. Our Lord carefully watches over those who call on Him and tends to our needs throughout every storm.

In the weeks before Hurricane Katrina hit New Orleans,

people casually strolled through the French Quarter, taking in the sights and enjoying the sounds of jazz. Then devastation struck. In the same way, before our tempest of grief hit, we may have felt secure and self-sufficient. Now we feel vulnerable and needy, painfully aware of the brevity and difficulty of life. Our heavenly Father invites us to humbly reach out for His secure and supportive arm. As the psalmist writes, He has compassion on those who acknowledge their weakness, just as an earthly father looks on his children's suffering with eyes of compassion.

Perhaps parenting analogies increase your pain, rather than offer you comfort. You may be grieving the death of your father. Or you may have no memories of a warm, loving dad. Then imagine an ideal father, or think of the parent you long to be. Ask God to open your eyes to see your gracious heavenly Father, who desires to hold you in His loving arms and gently wipe your tears.

"The Lord is compassionate and gracious, slow to anger, abounding in love" (Psalm 103:8). As you grieve this terrible loss in your life, His heart is filled with compassion for you. Through His presence, His Word, and His people, your Father reaches out to comfort you, His beloved child. Today may you find comfort in His loving embrace.

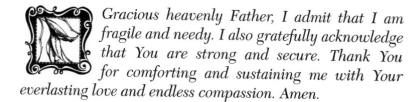
Gracious heavenly Father, I admit that I am fragile and needy. I also gratefully acknowledge that You are strong and secure. Thank You for comforting and sustaining me with Your everlasting love and endless compassion. Amen.

Embracing God's Comfort

Read through Psalm 103, listing the attributes of God that the psalmist includes. Now pray through your list, thanking God for His expressions of love and asking Him to open your eyes to see His compassion today.

_____

_____

_____

_____

_____

_____

_____

_____

_____

_____

_____

Broken Hearts Mended Here

*"The Spirit of the Sovereign Lord is on me....He has sent
me to bind up the brokenhearted, to proclaim freedom for
the captives and release from darkness for the prisoners...to
comfort all who mourn, and provide for those who grieve
in Zion—to bestow on them a crown of beauty instead
of ashes, the oil of gladness instead of mourning, and
a garment of praise instead of a spirit of despair. They
will be called oaks of righteousness, a planting of the
Lord for the display of his splendor." ~ Isaiah 61:1-3*

When the hospital staff took photographs of us holding our
dying son, I tried to smile. After all, I was cradling my precious
newborn—I should be happy. In reality, I was heartbroken,
so the pictures look ridiculous. David's and my forced smiles
sharply contrast with the unmasked sorrow reflected on our
older boys' faces.

In Isaiah's day the bereaved made no such effort to put
on a happy face. They literally wore their grief, covering
themselves with sackcloth and ashes. While others' faces
glistened with olive oil, reflecting their joy, those who
mourned looked downcast. They understood the value of
grieving fully.

But they also knew their time of mourning would pass.
Certainly they always would miss their loved ones, but they
knew that God offered comfort and would restore their joy.
He would replace their grief with a crown of beauty, the oil
of gladness, and a garment of praise.

God offers us the same comfort and restoration. We
who feel like weeping willows "will be called oaks of
righteousness, a planting of the Lord for the display of
his splendor." Our transformed lives will demonstrate the

healing impact of our Savior.

After our son's death, even acquaintances who did not yet know Jesus commented on the obvious effect of our faith. Because we trusted in God's sovereignty and our resurrection hope, we knew that Darren's brief life was not in vain. Thus, we could thank God for choosing us to help create this tiny baby, who would touch many hearts during his four short days and then glorify God in heaven throughout eternity.

People also recognized that, while our relationship with God did not eliminate our sorrow, it enabled us to bear the weight of it. Each day we depended on His strength and trusted in His faithfulness. We also looked to Him to restore us, and He far exceeded our expectations. Not only did our gracious Lord mend our broken hearts, but He also enlarged them, increasing our capacity to know and express His love and compassion. In this way and many others, He used our grief to nurture us as plantings "of the Lord for the display of his splendor."

Of course, oaks do not grow up overnight, and neither do we. We must patiently wait on God and allow ourselves ample time to grieve. Then, as we are ready, we can brush off our ashes and give God our despair. In exchange, He promises to graciously adorn us in beauty, gladness, and praise.

Today, whether you are wearing sackcloth or a simulated smile, rest assured that Jesus sees the depth of your pain. He who fulfilled this prophecy in Isaiah desires to lovingly put back together the pieces of your broken heart. In the midst of your grief, the Savior offers to comfort you and to restore to you the joy of life in Him as you grow through the nurture of His love.

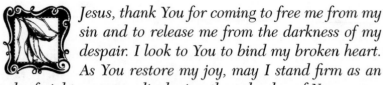*Jesus, thank You for coming to free me from my sin and to release me from the darkness of my despair. I look to You to bind my broken heart. As You restore my joy, may I stand firm as an oak of righteousness, displaying the splendor of Your grace and love. Amen.*

Embracing God's Comfort

Read Luke 4:14-21, then pour out your heart and pain to Jesus, who is the fulfillment of Isaiah 61:1-3. Ask Him to bind up your broken heart, comfort you, and restore your joy.

_____

_____

_____

_____

_____

_____

_____

_____

_____

_____

_____

PART THREE

Finding Comfort in God's Strength

"The Lord is my rock, my fortress and my deliverer; my God is my rock, in whom I take refuge. He is my shield…my stronghold."

~ Psalm 18:2 ~

Help, Lord! Save Me!

"The cords of death entangled me; the torrents of destruction overwhelmed me. The cords of the grave coiled around me; the snares of death confronted me. In my distress I called to the Lord; I cried to my God for help. From his temple he heard my voice; my cry came before him, into his ears….He reached down from on high and took hold of me; he drew me out of deep waters." ~ Psalm 18:4-6, 16

When our son Scott was two, we camped at the Oregon coast with several other families. On the last day, our group drove to the beach to build one final sand castle, which we then feverishly fought to protect from the incoming tide. Of course, the waves won.

As we walked back toward our cars, ready to head home, a friend ran up to David to hand him some towels we had left behind. At the same instant that he turned to take them, Scott stepped into what he thought was a very shallow tide pool and ended up totally submerged. He bobbed up once, then sunk again. No one from our group saw him, but fortunately a stranger did. Before David or I knew what was happening, this man jumped in and lifted our son out of the water. Scott was screaming and I was shaking and crying as we tried to thank the one who had saved his life.

Two years later, when Darren died, I felt as if I was the one drowning. I had been bound with the cords of grief and cast into a raging sea. It was all I could do to keep my head above the water. Like Scott, I floundered helplessly, lacking the strength to save myself. Fortunately, our ever-watchful Father was ready to rescue me.

Even the strongest among us face moments of total

helplessness. The psalmist David did. He had proved himself a mighty warrior when he defeated the giant Goliath, then victoriously led King Saul's troops in battle. Yet he grew weary of evading the king's unprovoked attempts on his life. "The torrents of destruction overwhelmed" him (Psalm 18:4). Despite his might, he knew he could not save himself, so he cried out to God for strength.

After Darren's death, people commended me for my apparent strength. Yes, at his memorial service I managed to read a poem without sobbing, but I attribute that to the initial numbness of grief and to my inhibitions about crying in public, rather than to any inherent strength. The stamina to live through the subsequent days of intense grief I credit only to the One I looked to throughout each day and ran to each night. After I tucked in Brent and Scott, I closed myself in our bedroom, knelt in prayer, and poured out my heart and tears. One hour and sixty tissues later, I felt like a puddle of Jell-O, but the Lord always remained as solid as a rock. As I emptied myself before Him, He filled me with His strength.

How reassuring to know that, no matter how weak and helpless we feel, God remains a strong fortress in whom we can take refuge. We need only call out to our deliverer. With power and majesty, He will come to rescue us, slashing through the "cords of death" that entangle us. Even if we feel like we are drowning in our despair, the psalmist assures us that God will reach down and take hold of us, drawing us "out of deep waters" (Psalm 18:16).

In the vulnerability of our grief, and throughout each day of our lives, may we trust in God's might. As David proclaimed, "Who is the Rock except our God? It is God who arms me with strength and makes my way perfect....You give me your shield of victory, and your right hand sustains me" (Psalm 18:31,32,35).

"I love you, O Lord, my strength" (Psalm 18:1). Thank You for being my rock, my refuge, my fortress. I call out to You to deliver me from the cords of grief that bind my soul. May I always draw upon Your strength to live each day. Amen.

Embracing God's Comfort

Read Psalm 18, noticing David's descriptions of God. Choose one word picture of God to contemplate. I invite you to close your eyes and picture Him delivering you from the pain of your grief.

I Think I Can't...I Think I Can't...

"I can do everything through him who gives
me strength." ~ Philippians 4:13

Do everything?! In those first months after our son's death, I barely had the motivation to boil water for a macaroni and cheese dinner or the energy to sort socks. Each day I struggled to meet my family's most basic physical and emotional needs, let alone "do everything."

Grief not only drained my husband and I of energy, but it also took its toll on our feelings of adequacy. David, who diligently worked to provide for and protect our family, faced his helplessness in shielding Darren from suffering and death and in consoling his remaining children and grief-stricken wife. At the same time, I felt incompetent as a woman, having "failed" to produce a healthy child. I even began growing my hair longer in an attempt to bolster my feelings of femininity.

Friends recognized our fatigue and sense of inadequacy. Some responded with meals or babysitting. Others reminded us it was legitimate and even best for everyone if we stepped back from previous commitments. While Philippians 4:13 promises God's strength for everything He asks us to do, it does not indicate that God asks us to do everything. We needed to recognize and accept our limitations, as well as to trust God to enable us to accomplish His will for us each day.

Even if we can diminish our load, walking the path of grief is physically exhausting. Crying itself leaves us feeling drained, not to mention dehydrated! When we sob, often our body shakes, we may gasp for air, and certainly every facial muscle is exercised. Mourning takes energy.

Unfortunately it is difficult to regain that energy because grief generally disrupts our sleep and diminishes our appetite. Our bodies are starving for rest and nutrition, yet we seldom can provide adequate amounts of either. Even as we begin taking better care of ourselves—eating well, exercising, resting—we still are exhausted by the end of the day.

Grief also drains us emotionally. As we move beyond our shock and denial, we must identify and express our feelings, such as sadness, abandonment, anger, anxiety, and guilt. We long for the ones whom death has stolen from us. We feel frustrated that we no longer can communicate our love to them, nor receive their love. We may find ourselves surprised, and perhaps embarrassed, at the intensity of our emotions and at our lack of control over them.

We also may feel self-conscious about how we vent our feelings. One day, in my struggle to accept Darren's death, I felt an overwhelming urge to yell, "No!" Not wanting my neighbors to hear me and call 911, I enclosed myself in our van in the garage and screamed "no" again and again, until I broke through my denial and into tears. Another day, at our school's carnival, I furiously threw darts at the balloon targets, which for me alone represented the enemy death. Another grieving mother bought dinner plates at a thrift store and threw them one by one at a board she had propped up on a tarp in her backyard. It provided a safe, albeit messy, release for her anger and grief.

Healthy expressions of our emotions promote healing, but they also can wear us out. During this time of grief, especially, we will benefit from nurturiing ourselves by taking time to think and read, to pursue hobbies or recreation, and to be with understanding friends.

Grieving also expends spiritual energy. We may question our belief in God, or at least how we feel about Him. Is he really sovereign and all-powerful? Does He truly love us?

Knowing that God could have kept Darren alive, but did not, I questioned His love. As I sought God through His Word and prayer, He strengthened my faith and deepened my understanding of His great devotion. I realized anew that He valued me enough to send His own beloved Son to die for me, that I might enjoy an eternal relationship with Him. He also cared enough to help me grow spiritually through my experience with my son's death. And, in love, God gave me the physical, emotional, and spiritual strength necessary for the lengthy grieving process.

How reassuring to know that we need not struggle through another day on our own; Jesus will carry us. As we acknowledge and accept our own inadequacy, we can draw upon the complete adequacy of God and live in His strength. He longs to live in us and empower us each moment of each day, for the rest of our lives.

Father, help me to be reasonable in my expectations of myself during this time of grief and to make efforts to nurture myself physically, emotionally, and spiritually. May I also look to You, knowing that You desire to share with me Your unending strength. Thank You that, as I rely on Jesus, I truly can do everything You call me to do. Amen.

Embracing God's Comfort

Do you need to withdraw from some obligations during this season of grief? Ask God for wisdom and the strength to say "no," as well as for the strength to accomplish each day's essential tasks.

_____

_____

_____

_____

_____

_____

_____

_____

_____

_____

_____

Our Shelter From the Storms

"God is our refuge and strength, an ever-present help in trouble. Therefore we will not fear, though the earth give way and the mountains fall into the heart of the sea, though its waters roar and foam and the mountains quake with their surging....The Lord Almighty is with us; the God of Jacob is our fortress." ~ Psalm 46:1-3,7

Living near Seattle, we are surrounded by mountains. Granted, much of the year we have to take that on faith, but on cloudless days I enjoy gazing at the Northwest Cascades, the Olympic Range, and majestic Mount Rainier. They appear steadfast, unconquerable.

Yet the 1980 eruption of nearby Mount St. Helens was a vivid reminder that not even mountains are immovable. Likewise, our nation is defenseless against the hurricanes that wreak havoc in the southeastern United States. Of course, the September 11, 2001 disintegration of New York's Twin Towers also left us all feeling vulnerable. And the death of a loved one certainly shakes us to the core. We indeed feel that the mountains have fallen into the sea, that our world has been turned upside down.

At such times we are especially aware of our need to hang on to the One who never changes. Our God stands sturdy, ready to be our refuge, our fortress. He longs for us to run to Him and to hide in the safety of His mighty, yet loving, arms.

The psalmist assures us that God is "an ever-present help in trouble. Therefore we will not fear." Death may sever us from those who always have been there for us or with whom we hoped and expected to walk through many more seasons of life. But death never can separate us from God. He is always with us, continually offering strength and security.

Watching our infant son die brought the reality of death into our home and left each of us feeling more vulnerable. As a mother, I had to guard against being overprotective of my then seven-year-old and four-year-old sons. I only would have heightened their fears had I capitulated to my own, so I tried to allow them the freedoms appropriate for their ages. I entrusted my second grader to the Lord as he ventured out on a school field trip to the aquarium and to investigate tide pools at the beach, fully aware that sometimes buses crash and children drown. With white knuckles, I prayed fervently as I watched him swinging high on a carnival ride (I admit, I also strategized how to catch him if he catapulted out). David and I did shield our boys from frightening movies and the evening news, however, as well as other sources of fear we deemed unnecessary.

We also tried to calm them when nightmares struck and to address their fears throughout the day. The world no longer felt as safe as it had before their brother died. We all felt more vulnerable, so we continually reminded our sons and ourselves that God remains steadfast. Daily we ran to Him for refuge, calling on Him to abide with us and to empower us.

When the seas are calm and the mountains stand firm, we might be tempted to put our trust in the things of this world. Even then, our only true security is in the One who created the heavens and earth, the mountains and the seas, our loved ones and all that we value. Throughout our lives, during times of peace and times of distress, strength comes from our Almighty God, who always remains with us. May we continually seek our refuge in Him.

Lord Almighty, I look to You as my refuge and strength in the midst of life's storms. May I also cling to You in times of peace, knowing that You desire my fellowship and my dependence. Thank You for always being there for me, and for always being here with me. I trust in You for the strength for today and each day. Amen.

Embracing God's Comfort

How has the death of your loved one affected your world or your perception of it? I invite you to write a description or draw a picture. Then describe or depict what God means to you at this time.

_____

_____

_____

_____

_____

_____

_____

_____

_____

_____

Life's Not Fair...Nor is Death

"My feet had almost slipped; I had nearly lost my foothold.
For I envied the arrogant when I saw the prosperity
of the wicked. They have no struggles; their bodies are
healthy and strong. They are free from the burdens
common to man; they are not plagued by human ills....
Yet I am always with you; you hold me by my right hand.
You guide me with your counsel, and afterward you will
take me into glory. Whom have I in heaven but you?
And earth has nothing I desire besides you. My flesh
and my heart may fail, but God is the strength of my
heart and my portion forever." ~ Psalm 73:2-5, 23-26

It doesn't seem fair. Why did God allow our friend Bob, who exercised regularly and never smoked a cigarette, to die at age forty-one of lung cancer? Why didn't He stop the drunk driver from ramming a Christian youth worker's car and stealing the lives of his two young daughters? Why was sixteen-year-old Sarah, who radiated Jesus' love, brutally murdered? And why does her killer remain free?

The psalmist Asaph wrestled with such questions. He faithfully followed God, yet encountered trial after trial. Meanwhile the wicked seemed to enjoy a carefree life. He goes as far as to say, "Surely in vain have I kept my heart pure" (Psalm 73:13).

Then, as Asaph worships in the sanctuary, God confirms that he has indeed made the right choice in following Him. Those who reject God may enjoy apparent peace and prosperity on earth, but those who love and obey Him will enjoy God's grace, blessings, and presence now and forever. Our abiding Savior and eternal destiny clearly overshadow our earthly experience.

Yet our earthly experience is very real—painfully real at times. It hurts terribly to lose someone we love. As I anticipated and then grieved the death of Darren, I felt as if my heart truly was breaking. At times the burden of sorrow was more than I could bear, had God not been "the strength of my heart."

I was grateful for God's presence and support, yet our son's death still felt unfair. I had surrendered to God my desire for another child, then discovered I was expecting. As with all my pregnancies, I had eaten healthily and avoided anything that might harm our unborn child. So why did my baby die? After joining the psalmist in his struggle with the apparent injustices in this life, I joined him as he clung to the Lord and to His promises of eternity with Him.

I also realized that I benefit from God's apparent unfairness. If He treated me as I deserve, I would be cast from His presence, rather than experiencing His love and blessings now and forever. I thanked Him that our relationship and His actions toward me are based on His grace, not my merit.

While I could express my adoration and appreciation, I still could not echo Asaph's words, "Whom have I in heaven but you? And earth has nothing I desire besides you." My son was in heaven, and I wanted him back! Yes, I desired God, but I longed for my child, too. And I certainly could not fathom having to say good-bye to my husband or other children. All these relationships were vitally important to me.

God helped me let go of my desire for Darren, and put my other relationships in their proper perspective, by reminding me of Abraham's willingness to sacrifice his own son (Genesis 22). He, who waited 100 years for an heir, expressed his love and devotion to God as he let go of his beloved son. Could I do the same? After again pouring out my heart to God in prayer, I surrendered Darren—and my will—to my gracious heavenly Father.

I am thankful for the loved ones I still have here on earth, and I believe that God wants me to enjoy my relationships with them. But I am striving to avoid an unhealthy devotion to or dependence upon them. My family and friends are important, but "God is the strength of my heart and my portion forever."

God, my strength, enables me to face the unfairness of life and death. His love and guiding presence sustain me when I suffer pain that I feel I don't deserve. And His graciousness keeps me going as I consider His abundant blessings, which I know I don't deserve.

Lord, give me the strength to deal with the apparent injustices on earth, including the loss of my loved one. Also help me to receive with gratitude Your gracious blessings. May I enjoy them, yet set my heart on You. Amen.

Embracing God's Comfort

Read Psalm 73. If you are struggling with the unfairness of life, express your frustration to God. Then ask Him to open your eyes to see what true fairness or justice is. Also ask Him to open your heart to His mercy and to the blessings and strength that He offers you now and for all eternity through a relationship with Him.

PART FOUR

Finding Comfort in the God of Hope

"Find rest, O my soul, in God alone;
my hope comes from him."
~ Psalm 62:5 ~

No Tissues in Heaven

*"Behold, I will create new heavens and a new earth.
The former things will not be remembered, nor will
they come to mind. But be glad and rejoice forever in
what I will create....the sound of weeping and of crying
will be heard in it no more. Never again will there be
in it an infant who lives but a few days, or an old man
who does not live out his years." ~ Isaiah 65:17-20*

A few days after his baby brother's death, Brent drew a picture of Darren on earth, with his eyes shut and his mouth turned slightly down. Then he portrayed Darren in heaven, healthy, happy, and surrounded by the bright yellow light of God's glory. Our seven-year-old son vividly illustrated the contrast between our fallen world and the perfect world to come, in which we place our hope.

When God first created the heavens and earth, He said that everything "was good" (Genesis 1:25). The Lord provided picturesque surroundings, fresh food, and meaningful tasks for the first person He formed. Adam also enjoyed good health and an unbroken relationship with his Creator. He lacked only one thing: companionship. "The Lord God said, 'It is not good for the man to be alone'" (Genesis 2:18). So God made Eve, and she and Adam experienced complete transparency with one another.

Despite their utopia, Adam and Eve soon rebelled against their Creator. Then, in shame, they tried to hide from one another and from God, but nothing in all creation could escape the consequences of their sin. Death entered the world, severing vital relationships and leaving behind broken hearts.

Fortunately, that is not the end of the story. As soon as sin and death invaded His creation, God offered life and hope to all who look to Him. In Genesis 3, He promised a Savior who would be victorious over sin, thus restoring our relationship with God and opening the door to eternity with Him. Then, in Isaiah 65, He gives us a glimpse of our heavenly home, which will be void of the intruder death.

I remember when my husband came upon this passage of Scripture in the months following our son's death. It verified our feelings that "it is not supposed to be this way." God created us for life, not for death. No wonder it hurt so much to be separated from our son. The verses validated the anger we felt toward death.

These promises also offered us tremendous hope. "Never again will there be in it an infant who lives but a few days, or an old man who does not live out his years." Death and sorrow are part of our fallen world; they will not be part of God's holy kingdom. We will again have unbroken relationships with one another, never to be severed by death. We also will experience a perfect relationship with our heavenly Father. That description of heaven filled our hearts with the hope we needed to endure our grief.

One summer we backpacked with another family into a mountain lake. They had hiked in before and assured us it was worth the trip. Having that hope helped us persevere up the rocky trail and even cross a slippery snow patch. When we finally reached the top and pried off our packs, we stood in awe of our breathtaking surroundings and the peacefulness of God's creation. Our friends were right; we were not disappointed.

How much more will this journey to heaven be "worth the trip." Certainly this life is painful and extremely difficult at times as we face suffering and death. But we can find strength for these trials as we hope in God and the joy we will experience in His eternal—and tissue-free—kingdom.

Jesus, I praise You as my Hope. My lifetime on this earth includes suffering and grief, as well as love and joy. Thank you that You promise an eternity without tears, without grief. I look forward to enjoying Your presence and everlasting fellowship with others. While I am here, help me to keep sight of my hope in You and to even share it with others. Amen.

Embracing God's Comfort

Write down and share with God what you are struggling with on earth and what you are looking forward to in heaven, His tissue-free kingdom.

Hope for the Hopeless

"Why have you rejected me? Why must I go about mourning...? Send forth your light and your truth, let them guide me; let them bring me to...the place where you dwell....Why are you downcast, O my soul? Why so disturbed within me? Put your hope in God, for I will yet praise him, my Savior and my God." ~ Psalm 43:2-5

When death stole Darren from us, I echoed the psalmists' cry. "Why have you rejected me, God? What did I do to deserve this devastating loss?"

Knowing that I had failed God repeatedly, I suspected that Darren's death was God's rod of punishment. I dredged up past sins, dragged them before the Lord and asked, "Is this why you took Darren?"

Then God sent His light, showing me that I was putting my hope in myself, rather than in Him. Would I dare to parade my "good works" before God and ask, "Have these good deeds earned me my wonderful husband, our other sons, a loving family, friends, and the many blessings in my life?"

No, I knew that everything I enjoy is a gift from God. And, while godly living and sin both have consequences, I concluded that my failings were not responsible for my son's death.

I still could not answer the "why," nor did I like my circumstances, but I put my hope in God, remembering His goodness, His love, His faithfulness. With pain in my heart and tears in my eyes, I joined the psalmists in praising my Savior and my God, my light, my joy, my hope.

Talking to God about our pain is one way to find hope. Talking to ourselves—our souls—is another. We can join the psalmists in asking, "Why are you downcast, O my soul?"

Six months after her husband died of cancer, author and speaker Dee Brestin said, "I have been talking to my soul when I get downcast."

When she felt lonely and afraid, she asked, "Soul, don't you remember when John was a prodigal at the age of 16 and God turned him around overnight? Soul, don't you remember when we prayed that I would be able to talk to my dad one last time when he was in that coma before he died, and I walked into his room and he opened his eyes?"[1]

Having studied and written about the psalms, Dee knew how to put her hope in God. Recalling His faithfulness in the past helped her trust Him with her present sorrows and future uncertainties.

Though we may feel abandoned by God, He is with us. Even when we are discouraged and distressed, He is our hope. As we turn to Him, He will send His light, His truth, and even His joy.

"Put your hope in God, for I will yet praise him, my Savior and my God."

God, my hope, You know I struggle with this tremendous loss in my life. I have felt wounded and rejected. In the midst of my pain, I have put my hope in myself—if only I had done this or had not done that. I have put my hope in my loved one—if only he or she were still here with me. I have hoped in my circumstance—if only I could have escaped this tragedy. Help me to instead put my hope in You, my faithful, unchanging, loving God. Amen.

Embracing God's Comfort

Are you feeling betrayed by God or by your loved one? Openly express your feelings to God. Then ask Him to be your hope. Invite Him to help you understand what it would look like today to trust in Him. How would your life look different?

As you seek to hope in God, remind yourself—your soul— of ways that God has taken care of you in the past, even if you did not recognize His hand at the time. When you feel ready, thank Him that He will continue to be faithful in the future.

_____

_____

_____

_____

_____

_____

He Has Prepared a Place

*"Do not let your hearts be troubled. Trust in God; trust
also in me. In my Father's house are many rooms; if it
were not so, I would have told you. I am going there
to prepare a place for you. And if I go and prepare a
place for you, I will come back and take you to be with
me that you also may be where I am." ~ John 14:1-3*

As soon as we walked in the door with our newborn son
Scott, two-year-old Brent eagerly narrated a guided tour of
the house. He then proudly held up his treasured toys, one
at a time, for his baby brother's inspection. Clearly, he joined
David and I in joyously welcoming Scott into our home and
family.

Four years later, both boys excitedly anticipated the arrival
of another baby. They helped me prepare the nursery, which
we decorated with curtains and wall hangings I had made for
each of them. They giggled as we unpacked baby clothes and
looked forward to helping dress their little brother (diaper
changing, however, they vowed to leave to Mom and Dad).
They could hardly wait to hang the "It's a Boy!" banner in the
front window of our house.

Then Darren was born, and my husband faced the daunting
task of explaining to Brent and Scott that their baby brother
would never come home, but instead would soon die.
Naturally, they were confused. It did not fit with their picture
of this world any more than it did with ours. Scott responded,
"But only old people die."

"Usually only old people die," David agreed. "But something
is wrong with Darren and he can't live."

Scott thought for a moment, then his face brightened a bit.
"Darren will be the first person in our family to see Jesus."

While Scott was very disappointed that his baby brother could not come to the house we had prepared for him, he found comfort and hope in knowing he would be at the home the Lord had made ready in heaven. If Darren had to die, at least he would soon see face to face the Jesus we all loved.

As I stand in our church services singing, I sometimes think of Darren, my father, and other loved ones standing before God's throne singing His praises. I find great comfort in knowing that they are in our heavenly Father's presence and care. And while I enjoy our home here on earth, I can only imagine the glory and splendor of their mansions.

Each year we choose a way to commemorate the anniversary of our son's birth and death. One year we gave to a charity in his honor. Another year we released five helium balloons: a red, representing our love for him; a blue, because we're sad he is not here with us; a green, representing his eternal life; a gold for the glory of heaven he now enjoys; and a white, because he is pure and sinless, with a perfect body.

On the sixth anniversary of his birth, we chose to release a single red "happy birthday" balloon, on which we wrote greetings expressing our love. The next day four-year-old Daniel, who was born after Darren, asked where the balloon was now. I said that it had gone very high in the sky. Scott, at age ten, pragmatically added that it had popped. Daniel seemed to know better. He shook his head and said, "I think Jesus grabbed it and gave it to Darren."

I would like to think that Daniel is right. Even if he is not, I'm thankful that he already knows that Jesus loves and takes care of His children. He takes care of us while we are here on earth, and He is preparing an eternal home for all who love Him and desire to dwell with Him. Darren and others who have gone before us have the finest of homes and are basking in God's presence. Perhaps some of them are even playing with helium balloons.

Jesus, You know I desperately miss my loved one. Thank You for Your comfort and for the hope You give in Your promise to prepare for us a glorious and eternal dwelling. Thank You, too, for giving Yourself as the way to our heavenly home. My hope is in You, my loving Savior. Amen.

Embracing God's Comfort

Close your eyes and envision the home that God is preparing for you. Imagine being reunited with loved ones and dwelling in the presence of the Lord. Draw or describe the pictures that come to your mind.

_____

_____

_____

_____

_____

_____

_____

_____

_____

_____

Eternally Secure Treasures...
Guaranteed

"Praise be to the God and Father of our Lord Jesus Christ!
In his great mercy he has given us new birth into a living
hope through the resurrection of Jesus Christ from the
dead, and into an inheritance that can never perish,
spoil or fade—kept in heaven for you." ~ 1 Peter 1:3-4

When my friend Laura gazed down at her ring, her heart sank. The pearl had fallen out. Seven Christmases ago her husband had given Laura this special ring with their daughter's birthstone as a remembrance of Sarah, who had been killed just days earlier. Now this memento was gone as well.

In time, precious keepsakes get lost, stolen, or broken. Our instant photos of Darren already have faded. Even memories wane. Eight years after her teenage daughter's death, Laura shared with me, "I have forgotten the sound of Sarah's voice, the smell of her hair, the sound of her step on the stairs."

Such losses remind us that eventually all our treasures on earth will fade, spoil, or perish. Economic crisis or medical bills quickly can deplete our financial resources; fire or flooding can destroy our sentimental treasures. And death already has torn away from us people we hold dear.

Our grief is multiplied if we were counting on these treasures as our hope in this life. Thus the apostle Peter reminds us in the verses above that we have a hope beyond this world—a living hope through Jesus' resurrection and an invincible inheritance. Our relationship with God and our spiritual treasures will never perish, spoil, or fade. They will remain safe and secure in God's kingdom until we are ushered in to fully embrace these eternal riches.

Jesus also pointed out the importance of our heavenly treasures and their effect on our earthly lives. "Where your treasure is, there your heart will be also" (Matthew 6:21). Recognizing the spiritual riches awaiting me in heaven, as well as the treasure of Darren and other loved ones who have gone before me, has helped me realize how briefly we all walk this earth. As another couple shared, after their baby died they have been much more mindful that this world is not their home. Someday they, too, will be home with Jesus and their son, enjoying the incomparable blessings that God has stored up for them.

Does this all mean that nothing on this earth matters to us? No, during our stay on earth, God invites us to enjoy the material and relational blessings He pours out. We are to delight in them, but not depend upon them. Our hope is in God and the blessings of His kingdom. God also expects us to grieve our losses in this world, as Jesus mourned Lazarus' death. But in our grief, we have hope in God and His kingdom.

Whatever losses we experience in this life, we can bank on our eternal relationship with God and the riches He has stored up for us to enjoy for all eternity. As His beloved children, we can anticipate receiving His inheritance, which never will deteriorate and cannot be stolen from us. In Christ, God has given us this living and lasting hope. Guaranteed.

Gracious Father, may I find comfort and hope in my relationship with You and all its blessings. Thank You for protecting my inheritance until I enter Your everlasting kingdom and receive these spiritual treasures. May I find strength for today in my eternal hope. Amen.

Embracing God's Comfort

Read Ephesians 1:3-11, noting our treasures in Christ. Take a moment to thank Him for these eternal, imperishable treasures.

_____

_____

_____

_____

_____

_____

_____

_____

_____

_____

_____

PART FIVE

Finding Comfort
in the
God of Peace

"And he will be called Wonderful
Counselor, Mighty God, Everlasting
Father, Prince of Peace."
~ Isaiah 9:6b ~

God's Presence Brings Peace

*"Peace I leave with you; my peace I give you. I do not
give to you as the world gives. Do not let your hearts
be troubled and do not be afraid." ~ John 14:27*

"And they lived happily ever after." As children, we smile
contentedly as we hear this over and over again. Then we grow
up, and we discover that life does not follow the storybook
pattern. Sometimes the dragons win.

Todd Beamer had no idea that "dragons" awaited him on
Flight 93 on September 11, 2001. He boarded the airplane
expecting just another business trip. Instead, he and other
passengers bravely prevented terrorists from turning the
airplane into a weapon of mass destruction. But this time the
heroes died; their families grieved.

Our family's story certainly took an unexpected turn when
Darren was born. During my pregnancy, excessive amniotic
fluid had caused some concern, but medical tests indicated
that all was well. The results gave us peace of mind; everyone
expected us to have a healthy baby and live happily ever after.
Instead, Darren's chapter in our lives lasted only four days.
Our family was heartbroken.

Ten years later, another "dragon" attacked our family. My
husband experienced disturbing symptoms, including the
loss of his reflexes and some strength on his left side. Again,
extensive tests offered reassurance by ruling out several
life-threatening conditions. This time we knew not to rely
on medical results, however, or any other peace the world
offers. Such peace can be shattered in a moment. Only our
assurance that God is with us and is in control could calm our
anxieties.

When Jesus addressed His disciples the night before His

crucifixion, they were experiencing a seemingly unhappy ending. These men had abandoned their professions to follow Jesus, expecting Him to bring their nation peace and freedom from Roman tyranny. With Jesus' pronouncement of His death sentence, however, this hope of world peace was ripped away, as was any personal peace of mind. As His close associates, they feared for their own lives and nation, as well as for their beloved Lord.

Jesus calmed His disciples' troubled and fearful hearts by promising that He would leave them with the only true peace: God's peace. He also assured them that He was not leaving them alone, but was giving them the Holy Spirit, the Counselor, the Comforter, who would live in them and thus be ever-present (John 14:16,17,26). Jesus taught that true peace is not the absence of conflict or trials—it is not "living happily ever after." Instead, true peace is God's presence with us in the midst of good times and hard times.

Richelle experienced this truth. Doctors offered no happy ending for her husband's yearlong battle with cancer, but she found peace in God's nearness. Family and friends had been a tremendous support, and she knew they would help see her through the days, months, and years ahead. She also knew that God would walk with her as she lived without her husband and raised her young children without their father. The assurance of His presence gave her the strength and serenity to say good-bye, to tell her suffering husband they would be OK. He did not need to keep fighting. She gave him the freedom to die in peace, knowing that she would live in peace. Yes, the pain would seem unbearable at times, but God's presence would see her through. And it has, day by day.

As we grieve our losses and fear the future in the absence of our loved ones, the world may try to offer peace and comfort. But true serenity comes from the presence of our risen Savior. His Spirit will always live in those of us who have invited Him into our hearts. As we pour out to Him our fears and rest in His presence, He will fill us with His comforting peace.

 Jesus, thank You for Your gift of peace, which comes through Your presence in my life and the promises in Your Word. As I suffer difficulties and grieve losses, calm my troubled and fearful heart and fill me with Your perfect peace. Amen.

Embracing God's Comfort

Are you feeling troubled by the pain of your present loss or the fear of your uncertain future? Ask God for the gift of His perfect peace. Spend time reading His written Word, listening to Him. In prayer, share your fears and requests. Find comfort and serenity in His presence, through His indwelling Spirit. Remember, Jesus is near to you.

_____

_____

_____

_____

_____

_____

_____

To Know Him is to Trust Him

"Grace and peace be yours in abundance through the knowledge of God and of Jesus our Lord." ~ 2 Peter 1:2

Shortly after we relocated in another state, our sons ran out of their Sunday school classes clutching summer camp applications and pleading, "Can we go?" Before our move, they had slept at friends' houses, but this was their first opportunity to spend three nights away from home. They were eager to swim in the lake, catch fish, and eat candy bars ten minutes before dinner.

While I was glad they felt comfortable enough to embark on this adventure, I found myself hesitant to sign on the dotted line. As much as I liked our new church and respected the leadership, I had not even met the men who would serve as counselors. Given the unsettling news stories that greet us each day, could I entrust my eight- and ten-year-old sons to strangers?

By the time next year's applications came home, I felt much more at home in our community and church. I certainly did not know everyone in our large congregation, but I trusted those who were investing their lives in our children. As Brent and Scott stepped on the camp bus that summer, my only concern was that they would never uncap their toothpaste tubes.

Generally, the deeper the relationship, the greater the trust. We feel safe with people we know and love and who have demonstrated their devotion and loyalty. In the same way, our confidence in God grows with our knowledge of Him; thus we experience peace in His presence and care.

As in any relationship, we achieve greater intimacy with our Creator and Lord through time and honest communication.

Reading the Bible, His love letter to the world, opens my eyes to my incredible Lord. I witness God's mercy toward Rahab the prostitute; King David the adulterer and murderer; and the repentant thief on the cross. I see God's patience as He gives Jonah a second chance and Gideon a second sign. I recognize His faithfulness in providing food to the Israelites as they journeyed through the desert, and in protecting Paul from his enemies. I also see His compassion in Jesus' tears.

God's graciousness fills each page of His Word as He pours out rich blessings and invites people like me to know Him and serve Him. His sacrificial love shines forth from the cross, where His only Son, my Savior, gave His life to cleanse us from guilt and release us from death. And the Almighty's power radiates from the open tomb of the risen Christ, who conquered sin and death.

Talking to God also deepens my understanding of the One who calls me His beloved. Without pretense I approach my heavenly Father, assured that He cherishes me despite my flaws and is never surprised by my fears, doubts, and anger. In prayer I express my adoration, naming qualities I've seen in His Word. I share my struggles, my sorrow, my needs, and I confess my failings, my sins. I also thank my gracious God for answers to prayer and for specific gifts—family, friends, a home, health, and opportunities to serve Him in the power of His indwelling Spirit.

Then I seek His guidance. In silence I listen for His still small voice, impressing upon my mind His love and truth. Often His words soothe, sometimes they sting, yet even then He restores me with the salve of His grace.

Perhaps you long to know God more deeply and to experience the peace that accompanies such knowledge. Your Creator is eager to reveal Himself to you through His Word and honest prayer. Draw near to Him today, sharing your pain and grief, seeking His love and comfort. And as you grow in your knowledge of our Lord, may "grace and peace be yours in abundance."

Lord Jesus, thank You for giving me Your Word, and especially the record of Your time on earth, that I might see You. Continually draw me closer to You and open my eyes that I might know You, rest in Your hands, and find grace and peace in my relationship with You. Amen.

Embracing God's Comfort

One of my favorite books in the Bible is the book of John, which beautifully paints a portrait of Jesus. Read a chapter each day, noting the words used to describe the Lord.

_____

_____

_____

_____

_____

_____

_____

_____

_____

_____

Exchanging Our Pain for His Peace

*"The Lord is near. Do not be anxious about anything, but
in everything, by prayer and petition, with thanksgiving,
present your requests to God. And the peace of God, which
transcends all understanding, will guard your hearts
and your minds in Christ Jesus." ~ Philippians 4:5-7*

"Your baby could have lived, but you took him off the
machine because he was brain-damaged," our friends' young
daughter stated matter-of-factly as we both stood in the
kitchen during a social gathering.

"No, he could *not* live," I insisted, straining to push back my
tears. "Darren died when he was born. The doctors revived
him but his heart and lungs were failing. He had no hope."

A few moments later I pulled aside another friend.
Trembling, I asked if people thought that we let Darren
die because he was imperfect. Every doctor advised us to
remove him from the ventilator, as we were prolonging his
death, not his life. Our pastor agreed. After earnest prayers
for wisdom, we believed that it was time to release our son
into the care of His heavenly Father. Now, nearly two months
later, this young girl's innocent comment led me to question
our decision.

As I cried on my friend's shoulder, she assured me that
everyone knew that we loved Darren and had acted in his
best interests. Still, later that night while my body lay in bed,
my mind returned to the neonatal unit and relived the four
days of Darren's life and the moments of his death. Had we
done everything we could for our son? I again sought God's
peace.

As we grieve the loss of loved ones, our hearts and minds
are especially vulnerable to the attacks of doubts, questions,

and fears. Could we have prevented their death? Why did God allow this to happen? Did they know how much we loved them? How will we ever go on without them? Through prayer we find the peace of God necessary to defend against these piercing arrows.

The verses above remind us "the Lord is near," walking alongside us down this arduous path, always ready to listen. When the leach of anxiety sucks out our energy, health, peace, and contentment, He will gently detach it. We need only to ask, openly sharing our troubles and needs. While He may not remove us from difficulties, He promises to give us serenity in the midst of them.

The expectation of His incredible peace gives us reason to bring our requests to God "with thanksgiving." With appreciation we can give Him our hurts and needs, knowing that they are in good hands. We also can thank Him for the time we had with our loved ones, and for the many good gifts He has given us throughout our lives. Then we can express gratitude for His nearness. How amazing that the God who created the universe and holds all things together dwells within His children and longs to hear our every need.

In this time of grief, our needs may include grace and strength for each day. Financial concerns and additional responsibilities may weigh us down. Perhaps we need to seek God's help in forgiving those whose malice or negligence contributed to our loved one's death. We also can ask Him to heal our broken hearts and return joy and laughter to our homes.

Whatever our pain, anxiety, or needs, God invites us to bring them to Him. In exchange, He offers His peace, "which transcends all understanding" and shields our hearts and minds from the doubts and fears that assail us.

Thank You, Lord, for Your nearness and Your loving care. May I give You my anxieties and wrap myself in Your peace, knowing that You care about everything that concerns me. You hold my life in Your hands. Amen.

Embracing God's Comfort

Take a few moments to tell God everything that worries you. Thank Him for caring. Then envision Him reaching out with one hand to take your concerns and with His other hand to offer you His peace. Imagine releasing your worries to Him, then grabbing hold of His peace and placing it to stand guard over your heart and mind.

_____

_____

_____

_____

_____

_____

_____

_____

_____

_____

PART SIX

Finding Comfort in the God of Joy

"The joy of the Lord is your strength."
~ Nehemiah 8:10b ~

Waiting for the Sunrise of Our Joy

*"Weeping may remain for a night, but rejoicing
comes in the morning." ~ Psalm 30:5*

Have you ever tried to rush a sunrise? I imagine the prophet Daniel could not wait for the morning light to shine through the cracks in the lion's den so he could be released to proclaim God's faithfulness, as well as to breathe the fresh air. Jesus must have been eager for the Easter sunrise, which heralded His triumphant power over the tomb. And on those sleepless nights when our minds are flooded with memories, questions, sorrow, and fears, we long for dawn to free us, so we can distract ourselves through another day.

Each morning comes in its time, not ours. Just ask generations of eager children, who have tried to hasten the first glint of daylight so they can pull their groggy parents out of bed and begin tearing open Christmas packages. We all must wait for the dawn, knowing it eventually will break through the darkness.

During the gloominess of grief, however, we may wonder if the brightness of joy ever will truly return to our lives. The cloud of grief oppresses us. Even when our tears run dry, our hearts still weep and we cannot imagine rejoicing again. Yet, David assures us in Psalm 30 that the sun will again shine, as it did for him after He called upon God in his despair.

"But when?" we groan. In the morning. We must not expect ourselves to "dance and be glad" at midnight. Mourning comes before morning; our grief cannot be rushed.

When the darkness of grief first falls, we generally are in shock, disbelief, and denial. We long for the deceased and tend to withdraw from others. Eventually we acknowledge the reality of the loss, an important first step toward our healing.

As the night moves on and the numbness wears off, we commonly experience somatic distress and intense emotions, such as depression, anxiety, anger, despair, guilt, and hopelessness. To move through this time, we must identify and express our feelings. We especially benefit if we can share them with someone we trust. This also helps remove barriers of isolation and cynicism, which we tend to erect to protect us in our vulnerability.

One afternoon, about two months after Darren's death, I felt anger welling up within me and spilling out onto my children. After talking to God about it, I called an understanding friend and shared with her the rage I felt toward death. Feeling a need to further express my anger, I asked her to watch Brent and Scott for an hour while I took my tennis racket and some balls to the nearby school playground. With each slam of the ball against the wall, I released some of my anger toward the enemy death. When I returned home with our boys, I no longer felt controlled by my anger…just a little sore in my shoulder.

Lastly, as the intensity of our emotions subsides, we come to accept our loved one's death and begin to move on. This involves reestablishing social contacts, restructuring our dreams and plans in light of that person's absence, and adopting new roles and skills. Certainly we never forget or stop loving this one who was so special to us, but the memories bring less pain.[2]

As we move through these stages and steps, we notice a dim light on the horizon. The darkness is lifting, and the brightness of joy begins to filter into our hearts. It's not that we have "gotten over it"—we never get over it. But we have gotten through it. With God's grace, we have survived the dark night of weeping and are catching sight of the first rays of morning. We may even notice that we see God more clearly now than we did before night fell.

Morning dawns slowly, and at times the clouds will return to hide the sunlight. But the God who faithfully brings us through the dark of night also will see us through each day. He assures us that our weeping eventually will cease, but His joy will remain with us for all eternity.

 Father, during this dark period of grief, I look forward to when I will join the psalmist in declaring, "You turned my wailing into dancing; you removed my sackcloth and clothed me with joy, that my heart may sing to you and not be silent. O Lord my God, I will give you thanks forever" (Psalm 30:11-12). Thank You for Your presence with me in the night and for the joy You restore in the morning. Amen.

Embracing God's Comfort

How is grief affecting you? Where do you see yourself in the process and what will help you keep moving through your grief?

Finding Joy in the Midst of Pain

*"Though the fig tree does not bud and there are no grapes
on the vines, though the olive crop fails and the fields
produce no food, though there are no sheep in the pen
and no cattle in the stalls, yet I will rejoice in the Lord, I
will be joyful in God my Savior." ~ Habakkuk 3:17-18*

At age twenty-eight, my biological clock ticked loudly, but
the doctors could not explain our failure to conceive a child.
Would I never realize my dream of being a mother?

On my knees, I ranted and raved to God about His seeming
unfairness and apparent lack of love. How could He withhold
from me my heart's desire? It was not as if I wanted something
harmful or unreasonable. I simply wanted to experience the
blessing of loving and raising children.

After venting my anger and frustration, I realized that
God owed me nothing, not even a baby, and already He had
given me far more than I deserve. Even if I never received
another gift from His hand, I had ample reason to spend
eternity thanking and praising my gracious Lord. He had
given me life, my husband, family, friends, opportunities,
and countless material and spiritual blessings. Above all,
He had given me forgiveness and eternal life through Jesus
Christ my Savior. With Habakkuk, I chose to look beyond
my circumstances and to rejoice in God my Savior. I still was
not smiling from ear to ear, but I experienced contentment
in Him.

I soon realized that God not only is merciful and gracious,
but He also has a sense of humor. While I was pouring out
my tears and complaints, He was weaving in my womb a
precious baby. God already planned to give us our firstborn
son, but first He wanted to help me find my joy in the gift of

His one and only Son.

Two years later, I suffered spiritual amnesia and had to return to my "Joy in the Lord 101" classroom. Now doctors were saying my newly diagnosed medical condition made it best not to have any more children. It appeared that Brent would be an only child. I had nothing against only children—I married one—but I longed to nurture another child, as well as for Brent to have a sibling. Again I cried out to God, "If you loved me...."

Then I remembered. God already had proven His love over and over again. He owed me nothing else; He had not even owed me what He already had granted me. Though my circumstances were not ideal, I found joy in God my Savior. God then revealed that He already had granted my petition; Scott was growing in my womb.

My medical concerns subsided and, before Scott was speaking in sentences, my heart's desire for another child returned. This time I was to learn joy without the blessing of another baby. Again I thanked the Lord for my eternal relationship with Him. Jesus, my Savior, provided every reason to rejoice.

Content with our family of four, I assumed I had successfully completed my course. Then God handed me my most difficult test, which I hope was my final exam. In the past, I had grieved my unfulfilled desire for children and then found my joy in the Lord. Now I was grieving the loss of Darren, a child I had held and loved. Could I find contentment and joy in my gracious and faithful Savior this time?

I cried out to God, and again He opened my eyes to His boundless love. While I grieved deeply and still detested my circumstances, I would not succumb to them. My tears flowed, but I did not allow them to wash away my joy in Christ.

Though our loved ones are gone and our pain is immense, though our dreams are shattered and our future looks bleak, still we can join Habakkuk in finding joy in our God. We, too, can determine to rejoice in our Creator, our Lord, our Savior, who has proven Himself gracious and faithful. In Him we find unconquerable joy.

 Lord Jesus, You know I certainly would not choose these circumstances, but I do choose to find my joy in You. Thank You for this special person who has died, as well as for my other loved ones and for the many blessings You have poured out in my life. Most of all, thank You for dying for me that I might eternally rejoice in my relationship with the living God. Amen.

Embracing God's Comfort

In a verbal or written prayer, thank God for His presence and for His many blessings.

Joy in God's Presence

"Therefore my heart is glad and my tongue rejoices; my body also will rest secure, because you will not abandon me to the grave,...You have made known to me the path of life; you will fill me with joy in your presence, with eternal pleasures at your right hand." ~ Psalm 16:9-11

As his family crossed the Atlantic Ocean, their ship collided with another, and the sea swallowed his four daughters. Certainly Horatio Spafford's heart was broken. Yet as his tears flowed, so did his praise for His Savior. He knew that though his children's earthly bodies lay in their watery grave, their immortal bodies were safe in heaven, rejoicing in Jesus' presence and enjoying His abundant blessings. He also found comfort in his assurance that someday he would join them. Days after their death, he wrote these words, which became a beloved hymn:

> When peace like a river attendeth my way,
> When sorrows like sea billows roll;
> Whatever my lot, Thou has taught me to say,
> "It is well, it is well with my soul."[3]

In Psalm 16, David also expressed unwavering hope in God's eternal kingdom as he endured suffering in this world. Confident of God's presence with him now and forever, his heart was filled with gladness, his mouth with rejoicing. While he delighted in the blessings of this world, including loving relationships, he did not depend on them, but rather on the everlasting joy that only God provides. Thus, when trials and tragedy struck, though his heart ached, he remained secure in his eternal hope.

In grieving my precious son, I, too, was comforted in God's promise of eternal life. I have no doubt that our gracious

Father ushered Darren into His kingdom, as I believe He welcomes all those who have no opportunity to choose or reject the Savior. I share the confidence King David expressed after his infant son died: "I will go to him, but he will not return to me" (2 Samuel 12:23). King David later joined his son in heaven; someday I will join mine.

Until then, while I miss Darren, my heart is glad as I envision him praising God at His throne, filled with joy. I can only imagine all he enjoys in the presence of His heavenly Father, who is pouring out His abundant and eternal pleasures. I could ask for nothing better for my son.

Nor could I ask for anything more wonderful for myself. Knowing that, when my earthly life ends, I will be ushered into God's presence brings great comfort. Such hope strengthens me and fills my heart with joy despite life's circumstances. I thank God He has revealed to me "the path of life," which is Jesus Christ His Son.

Unfortunately, not everyone chooses the way to eternal life, so sometimes we grieve without the assurance that our loved ones are in heaven. We hope that at some point before their death they trusted in the Savior; God alone knows their hearts and eternal destiny. But we lack the comfort that accompanies confidence in their salvation. Nevertheless, we can rest assured of our own personal and everlasting relationship with the Lord. The apostle John wrote, "God has given us eternal life, and this life is in his Son. He who has the Son has life; he who does not have the Son of God does not have life. I write these things to you who believe in the name of the Son of God so that you may know that you have eternal life" (1 John 5:11-13).

With this confidence of our eternal destiny comes a peace and joy that cannot be taken away from us. Though death separates us from those in whom we delight on earth, nothing can sever our relationship with our Savior. In God and His kingdom we can find ultimate and everlasting joy, now and forever. Thus, we can join Horatio Spafford in saying, "Praise the Lord...it is well with my soul."

 Savior and Lord, thank You for inviting me to spend eternity in Your presence, experiencing the endless "pleasures at Your right hand." May this hope comfort and strengthen me in the midst of my sorrow. And may I find joy in You, even today, as I rest assured of Your promises for tomorrow. Amen.

Embracing God's Comfort

Share with God the difficulty of your circumstances. Then ask Him to help you find your joy in your relationship with Him.

What Time is It?

"There is a time for everything, and a season for every activity under heaven: a time to be born and a time to die,...a time to weep and a time to laugh, a time to mourn and a time to dance." ~ Ecclesiastes 3:1-4

Shortly after their baby girl died, our friends were invited to join some other couples to play Bunco. Rick felt ready for a night out and Diane thought it might raise her spirits as well. The other guests kept the conversation light, hoping to draw this grieving couple into the laughter and fun, but obviously their hearts were heavy. When the game finally ended, they graciously but quickly said their good-byes, closing their car doors with a sigh of relief.

As wise King Solomon observed in Ecclesiastes, there is a time to weep and mourn and a time to laugh and dance. That evening Rick and Diane realized that, while some of the intensity of their emotions had left, they were not yet ready to put on their dancing shoes.

Death ushers in a dreary season of winter in our lives, when life looks bleak and the simple pleasures elude us. It is a time to weep, to pour out our hearts to God in sorrow and prayer, to seek comfort in His Word and in supportive friends. It is a time to cry freely without apology, to grieve fully without pretense.

It also is a time that seems to last forever. After months of winter, we may wonder if spring ever will return. Just as each February we doubt that the clouds will part and the flowers will bloom, so we who grieve begin to question if the darkness ever will leave our hearts. We're not anticipating "getting over" the death of our loved ones; we know we always will miss them. Their lives and death have left an indelible mark on us. But we wonder if we truly will progress through the stages of grief and eventually come to a point when tears and sorrow subside.

Solomon assures us that we will. The hours pass, the seasons change. Our hearts become lighter and we recapture our enjoyment of life. Then one day something strikes us funny and we even chuckle, or at least involuntarily raise the corners of our mouth.

Our reaction, however, may surprise us. Rather than delighting in the novel experience, we may feel guilty. How can we laugh or even smile when someone we love has died? Our fleeting happiness is quickly squelched by a blanket of remorse.

Just as we must allow ourselves to cry and grieve, we need to permit ourselves to smile and laugh. We need not try to prove our love for those who died by donning sackcloth and ashes for the remainder of our lives. Certainly we need to fully mourn our loss, but we also can welcome back days of laughter and dancing.

As I mourned the loss of our son, the season of spring finally came. My tears flowed less frequently, and I was not continually weighed down with sorrow. I still experienced moments of sadness, such as when I saw children the age Darren would be, or a hospital helicopter like the one that had rushed him to the neonatal unit across town. And some days, for no obvious reason, the clouds of sorrow rolled back in. But generally I smiled more readily, laughed more frequently, and enjoyed the blessings of God still surrounding me.

We need not rush winter, nor resist spring. God will walk with us through each season and will use the sorrow as well as the gladness in our lives. As Solomon writes, "He has made everything beautiful in its time" (Ecclesiastes 3:11). May we find His beauty even in our grief and celebrate the returning days of laughter and dancing.

God, thank You for Your healing presence in this time of sorrow and Your hope-filled promise that I will laugh again. I look to You to see me through each season of my life. Amen.

Embracing God's Comfort

What time is it? If it is time to cry, then weep freely. If you feel ready to dance, do so without apology. Ask God to help you identify and accept the seasons of your grief.

_____

_____

_____

_____

_____

_____

_____

_____

_____

_____

_____

_____

PART SEVEN

Finding Comfort
in
God's Faithfulness

"The Lord is faithful to all his promises
and loving toward all he has made."
Psalm 145:13b ~

He Takes Care of the Orphans and Widows

"Blessed is he whose help is the God of Jacob, whose hope is in the Lord his God, the Maker of heaven and earth, the sea, and everything in them—the Lord, who remains faithful forever....The Lord watches over the alien and sustains the fatherless and widow." ~ Psalm 146:5-6,9

First, death had taken her husband, now drought had devastated her homeland. Her only remaining food was a handful of flour and a few drops of oil. Imagine this woman's despair as she gathered sticks for a fire so she could prepare one last meager meal for her son and herself.

Then God's prophet Elijah approached and asked her for a drink of water and a piece of bread. After the widow explained her plight, Elijah assured her that if she first made bread for him, God would continually fill her jar with flour and her jug with oil until the rains returned. She responded in faith, preparing Elijah's meal first, and "the jar of flour was not used up and the jug of oil did not run dry, in keeping with the word of the Lord spoken by Elijah" (1 Kings 17:16).

Another widow experienced God's faithful provision when she cried out in desperation to Elijah's successor, Elisha. All she had left were her two sons, and she soon would lose them to a creditor who planned to enslave them as payment for her outstanding debts. Elisha asked if she had anything else of value. "Nothing...," she said, "except a little oil" (2 Kings 4:2). The prophet then instructed her to gather from her neighbors as many jars as she could and pour into them the remaining oil. With wonder she filled jar after jar after jar after jar. Finally she ran out of oil, but only after the last container was full. Elisha then told her to, "Go, sell the oil and pay your debts. You and your sons can live on what is left" (2 Kings 4:7).

God faithfully and lovingly provides for the orphans and widows and others in need. He may not multiply our flour or oil, but He will sustain us as we call out to Him. He who created all things will care for His most valued creation—His people.

While my husband and I were not widowed or fatherless, we experienced God's faithfulness in our time of need. He generously provided the finances necessary to cover Darren's stay in the neonatal unit, as well as his burial expenses, and even threw in some extra for a much needed vacation several months later.

Throughout the first year of grief, God continued to encourage us through the prayers, timely notes of encouragement, and other expressions of emotional support from friends and family. He sustained our marriage as well. Grief resurfaced past hurts, added tension to our relationship, and left us with little to give to one another. As we looked to God and drew upon His grace, He held David and I together in His loving hands.

Richelle also saw God's faithful provision as friends and relatives rallied around them during her husband's unsuccessful battle with cancer. Family members have continued to express God's love by taking her son camping and providing male role models for both her children. Her Heavenly Father also has provided the finances, wisdom, and energy necessary to care for her family.

Jo Ann, whose husband also succumbed to cancer, knows that God is watching over her and meeting her needs. "I pray and, without fail, within hours He puts someone in my path who encourages me or provides exactly what I need."

After Jo Ann prayed about her need for a car, a dealer called her about a trade-in, which was priced at the exact amount she could afford. When she was struggling as a single parent and concerned about one of her teenagers' choices, a woman invited her to a Bible study that specifically addressed her needs. When Jo Ann has felt lonely, friends have called. She knows that her heavenly Father is watching over and taking care of her.

Another woman, while grieving the loss of her husband, found comfort and hope by beginning an eternal relationship with Christ. God did not take away Melanee's pain, but He helped her endure it as she rested in His loving arms. He also proved Himself dependable to meet her needs, often through His body, the church. Her young son, while missing his earthly father, discovered that his heavenly Father desired a personal relationship with him, a bond which death never will sever. Their lives testify of God's faithfulness.

Whatever our loss, we can find strength and comfort in remembering that God watches over us and sustains us. He who loves us more than we can even fathom, remains faithful forever, and faithfully remains forever with those who have put their hope in Him. May we trust Him to "give us today our daily bread" (Matthew 6:11) and to meet our every need.

Father, I call out to You who have proven Yourself faithful throughout history and in my life. I trust in You to sustain me and to provide for my needs now and forever. Thank You for Your immeasurable love and unending faithfulness. Amen.

Embracing God's Comfort

Have you seen God meet specific needs during this time of loss? Thank Him for His provision. What are your needs right now? Ask God to continue to meet your daily emotional, physical, relational, and spiritual needs.

_____

_____

_____

_____

_____

_____

_____

_____

_____

_____

_____

_____

God Will See Us Through

"No test or temptation that comes your way is beyond the course of what others have had to face. All you need to remember is that God will never let you down; he'll never let you be pushed past your limit; he'll always be there to help you come through it." ~ 1 Corinthians 10:13 (The Message)

"I know that God says He won't give us more than we can handle, but this time I think He did," one woman shared a few months after the death of her adult son.

She is not alone. I have yet to meet anyone who feels flattered that God deemed him or her strong enough to withstand this grueling test. Rather, we tend to wonder if He misjudged us. Dealing with death feels like too heavy a load to bear. This time God seems to be pushing us past our limits.

But the apostle Paul, who knew all about tests, wrote with confidence that God never allows us to face a trial we cannot withstand. Paul had endured floggings, imprisonment, beatings, stonings, a shipwreck, and numerous attempts on his life (2 Corinthians 11:23-29). He had come through each test knowing that God would not give him a burden heavier than he could bear.

Paul also knew, and assures us, that the God who superintends our suffering faithfully walks through it with us. He has laid out a pathway through our present trial and will gently guide us along the way. In the darkness of our grief, we cannot begin to see the end of the road, but we need only proceed one step at a time, trusting Him to see us through.

Strength for the journey comes from God, who holds our hand, and from others who have faced similar courses.

Their pain helps us accept the depth of our own grief; their endurance offers us hope as we witness God's faithfulness and healing in their lives. While even those who have lost loved ones dare not say, "I know just how you feel," they often listen without passing judgment and can empathize with our pain. Common threads run through each experience of loss.

One grieving mother hesitated to share her thoughts and feelings with others, fearing they would respond with criticism rather than understanding. Then, in the safety of a small support group for grieving mothers, she courageously and tearfully poured out her heart, sharing painful details of her child's death. This prompted the woman seated next to her to respond with her story, which nearly mirrored the first. Both women found great solace in knowing they were not alone. Someone else had walked an almost identical path, which comforted and strengthened both of them for their still painful journeys.

You may wish to seek support with a group of others who have faced losses similar to your own. If you cannot find such a group, perhaps someone in your church or another nearby church would be willing to start one. The first group I led resulted from such a request. While no one can take away your pain, others who grieve can help you bear it as they listen with understanding and acceptance.

We also find strength and comfort in knowing that God understands and accepts us in our suffering. As Paul wrote, He never will let us down and will always stay with us, helping us through our grief. May we live each moment trusting in His faithfulness and following His leading.

Faithful Father, sometimes I wonder if this time You truly did give me more than I can handle, but I trust in Your promise that You know my limits. I also trust You to guide me through this time of grief. May I find support in Your presence and in the example and understanding of others who have faced similar trials. Amen.

Embracing God's Comfort

Do you feel like God has given you more than you can handle? Write down your thoughts and feelings. Also, consider joining a support group for those who have experienced the loss of a loved one. Often people are a part of God's provision and a means of expressing His comfort and compassion. (See page 143 for suggestions for using this book in a group setting.)

_____

_____

_____

_____

_____

_____

_____

_____

Remember Me, God?

*"For the Lord comforts his people and will have compassion
on his afflicted ones. But Zion said, 'The Lord has forsaken
me, the Lord has forgotten me.'
'Can a mother forget the baby at her breast and have
no compassion on the child she has borne? Though she
may forget, I will not forget you! See, I have engraved
you on the palms of my hands.'" ~ Isaiah 49:13-16*

I remember the first time our family watched the movie
Home Alone. Our sons delighted in the self-preservation
antics of young Kevin, who mistakenly was left behind when
his family flew to Europe for Christmas. I, on the other hand,
identified with the distraught mother who cried out that she
was desperate enough to hitchhike on the runway, or to give
up everything she owned, if that was what it took to fly back
home to her abandoned son.

Most parents love their children and strive to nurture and
protect them. Their hearts break when their children suffer
and they rejoice when they succeed. Mothers and fathers
generally do their best to meet their children's needs and to
keep them safe.

Yet, even dedicated parents sometimes fail. While I never
have forgotten to take them on a vacation, I have neglected
to follow through on commitments to my sons. I always
remember their names, but sometimes I go through every
other name in the family (including the dog's) before I get
to the right one. And I recall dozing off a few times while
nursing, seemingly forgetting the baby at my breast.

God assures us that, while we who lovingly dote on our
children may occasionally let them down, He is faithful and
never will fail us. He is a perfect parent to each of us, never

neglecting those whom He created and has engraved on the palm of His hand. How can He forget us for whom He sent His Son to die?

When tragedy strikes, however, we may feel as if God has abandoned us. I remember calling out after Darren's death, "Hey, Lord, remember me? The one You just stepped on?"

I did not understand why God had allowed my son's death. Through my suffering, however, I came to a deeper understanding of His care and compassion. He had not stepped on nor neglected me, but rather was holding me in His loving arms and carrying me through my grief. In my sorrow and weakness, I came to a greater appreciation of His compassion and strength.

God also opened my eyes to His faithfulness. Even when it seemed that others had forgotten my loss, my heavenly Father demonstrated that He—and others—did remember. One difficult day, I received an encouraging note in the mail from an acquaintance. Five months after Darren's death, when a close friend gave birth to her healthy baby, a neighbor brought by a plate of brownies. She understood that my joy for their family was mixed with sorrow for my loss. God also faithfully encouraged me through Bible verses that would speak to my specific needs.

As long as we live in this fallen world, we will experience pain and sorrow. But we also can know God's comfort and compassion. We are not alone; we are not forgotten. In our grief we can trust in our faithful Father.

Ever-present Father, when I feel abandoned by You, may I trust in Your loving care, knowing that You never could forget the children whom You created and then restored to a love relationship through Your Son. May I find comfort and compassion in Your unfailing love. Amen.

Embracing God's Comfort

Close your eyes and envision your faithful and loving heavenly Father watching you and reaching down to help you. If you feel ready, express to Him your appreciation and love.

_____

_____

_____

_____

_____

_____

_____

_____

_____

_____

Seeing God Through Our Tears

*"My ears had heard of you but now my
eyes have seen you." ~ Job 42:5*

Job had it all—wealth, family, prestige. No doubt *Time
Magazine* would have voted him "Man of the Year." Even
more impressive, he was esteemed by God, who said, "There
is no one on earth like him; he is blameless and upright, a
man who fears God and shuns evil" (Job 1:8).

Then one day his life and world were turned upside down.
First, Job learned that all of his 11,000 livestock had been
stolen or destroyed, and his numerous servants were dead.
Moments later he was told that his son's house collapsed,
instantly killing Job's ten children. In this one terrible day,
nearly all that he valued was ripped from his hands.

Upon hearing this devastating news, Job openly expressed
his grief by tearing his robe and shaving his head. Then he
"fell to the ground in worship and said: 'Naked I came from
my mother's womb, and naked I will depart. The Lord gave
and the Lord has taken away; may the name of the Lord be
praised'" (Job 1:20-21).

Job's faithful response did not surprise God, but it frustrated
Satan, who was attempting to turn Job against the Lord. Not
one to give up easily, the devil tried another tactic. He afflicted
this poor grief-stricken man with painful sores from head to
toe. Figuring enough was enough, Job's wife then urged him
to let go of his integrity, which seemingly had not done him
much good, and to "curse God and die!" (Job 2:9).

Job knew better, because he knew the Lord. "He replied,
'You are talking like a foolish woman. Shall we accept good
from God, and not trouble?'" (Job 2:10). He realized that
God was not obligated to protect him from all pain. But that

did not mean he welcomed his suffering. In chapter three, we read that Job wished he had died at birth, rather than endure the pain of this life.

Yet despite these tragedies and the added torment from his wife and friends, whom he calls "miserable comforters" (Job 16:2), Job continues to trust in God and His faithfulness. He finds that God is faithful to lovingly stay with him throughout his suffering and to reveal Himself in the midst of life's tragedies. Grief and pain opened Job's eyes to see God as his Creator and the sovereign Lord.

While my loss was not as extensive as Job's, I, too, found that grief enabled me to see God more clearly and to know Him more deeply. I experienced His loving faithfulness to see me through the most difficult days, weeks, months, and year of my life. His amazing grace became much more than a song as He accepted my anger toward Him and continually held me in His tender care. He also opened my tear-filled eyes to His lordship and eventually enabled me to embrace His sovereignty as an expression of His love, even when it meant He had allowed the death of one I loved.

During our years on earth, we never can fully know or comprehend God. As Paul writes, "Now we see but a poor reflection as in a mirror; then we shall see face to face. Now I know in part; then I shall know fully, even as I am fully known" (1 Corinthians 13:12). For now we must settle for a muddled reflection.

But someday we will see God face to face, in all of His splendor. I expect that His undiminished glory will dispense any questions of why He allowed pain during our journey on earth. Until then we can trust Him to see us through our grief and to use our suffering, as He used Job's, to reveal a clearer reflection of our faithful, gracious, loving, and sovereign Lord.

Lord, You are beyond my comprehension, but I thank You for revealing Yourself to me through Your Word and Your works, including Your people. May I see You more clearly as I draw near to You during this very difficult time. And may I trust in Your love and faithfulness each day. Amen.

Embracing God's Comfort

Read and reflect on the picture of God presented in Psalm 103. You may wish to write down the characteristics of God. I also invite you to pray the psalm in your own words. For example, from verse 4, "You have saved me from eternal death and crowned me with Your love and compassion."

_____

_____

_____

_____

_____

_____

_____

_____

_____

_____

Refining Our Faith

"Now for a little while you may have had to suffer grief in all kinds of trials. These have come so that your faith—of greater worth than gold, which perishes even though refined by fire—may be proved genuine and may result in praise, glory and honor when Jesus Christ is revealed." ~1 Peter 1:6-7

While I recognize the monetary value of even a small gold nugget, I might not ooh and aah if my husband wrapped one up for me for our anniversary. However I cherish his gifts of a polished gold heart necklace, a braided gold bracelet, and a delicate serpentine gold ring, as well as my wedding band. Each has survived the refining process that separated out the dross; each has withstood the intense heat that enabled the remaining precious metal to be skillfully molded into an exquisite piece of jewelry.

The apostle Peter assures us that, when placed on the scales, our faith far outweighs even the finest gold and becomes exceedingly more glorious as it endures the refining fire. Our confidence in God in the midst of our suffering proves and strengthens our faith and displays His trustworthiness. Affliction also removes from our lives some of the dross, the hindrances to knowing and serving our Lord.

Of course, the furnace of suffering brings excruciating pain as well, and we wonder why God could not at least have handed us an asbestos suit on the way in. Peter assures us that He has. Wherever we are, we "are shielded by God's power" (1 Peter 1:5). Certainly we feel the heat, but the flames will not consume us or the blessings of our eternal relationship with God.

Shadrach, Meshach, and Abednego experienced God's

faithful protection when they refused to worship a golden statue of King Nebuchadnezzar. Furious, the king had them bound and cast into a blazing furnace, which was so hot it instantly killed the arresting soldiers. Then the king watched in amazement as Shadrach, Meshach, and Abednego walked around in the furnace, unharmed and joined by a heavenly being. King Nebuchadnezzar quickly called them out and "saw that the fire had not harmed their bodies, nor was a hair of their heads singed; their robes were not scorched, and there was no smell of fire on them" (Daniel 3:27). Only the ropes were burned, releasing them from bondage.

As a result of this trial, the king and the other rulers who witnessed God's protection and presence praised God, recognizing that "no other god can save in this way" (Daniel 3:29). Of course, Shadrach, Meshach, and Abednego entered the furnace already confident of God's saving ability. They also were assured that, even if their physical bodies and possessions perished, their relationship with God and spiritual riches remained safe and secure. No doubt they walked out of the furnace with an even stronger faith in God's shielding power and constant presence. Rather than burning them, the fire had blessed them and freed them.

Job, too, expressed confidence in God's presence as well as in the refining benefits of his trials. In the midst of his suffering he desperately searched for God, apparently without avail. Still he knew that God never lost sight of him and would be pleased with Job's unwavering trust. "I do not see him;...I catch no glimpse of him. But he knows the way that I take; when he has tested me, I will come forth as gold" (Job 23:9,10).

While not physically visible to us either, God certainly walked with my husband and me as we anguished over whether or not our son would live, and then struggled to say good-bye. He also clearly used the fire of our affliction to help transform our lives. I hated the agony of the flames, but if that is what it took to cleanse and transform me, then I embraced their work in my life. I desired for God to be glorified as He melted me, skimming off some of my self-centeredness, and molded me into a more compassionate individual with increasingly eternal values. I also longed to display God's glory to others as He demonstrated His faithfulness in our time of need.

I am not yet a glistening gold pendant, but God is not finished with me. For now He has turned down the flame, but He continues to purge, shape, and polish me through daily opportunities to trust Him. In the future He may even walk me through another fiery furnace. While I will not welcome the distress, I desire the purification and refinement, so that I might shine more brightly for Christ.

In the midst of our trials, may we remember that God values each of us and our faith far above any precious metal. Whether we are being melted in the furnace or molded on the anvil, He is refining and beautifying His beloved treasures. And He remains with us each step of the process. May we find comfort in His presence and joy in reflecting His radiance and glory.

 *Father, thank You for faithfully walking with me and protecting me in the furnace of my affliction. Continue to give me grace as I suffer through my grief—the flames hurt! But use them to transform me for Your glory. May others see Your faithfulness in my life and join me in desiring to glorify You. Amen.*

Embracing God's Comfort

Write down any ways you are seeing God refine you through this trial. Ask Him for His grace and strength as He continues this process.

_____

_____

_____

_____

_____

_____

_____

_____

_____

_____

_____

PART EIGHT

Finding Comfort in God's Love

The Lord says, "I have loved you with an everlasting love."
~ Jeremiah 31:3b ~

God's Unfailing Love

"We know and rely on the love God has
for us. God is love." ~ 1 John 4:16

A week after we moved into our thirty-year-old home, an icy December storm knocked out our power for four days. Our family of five camped out in the one room with the wood stove, which also happened to be the room in which we had piled our unpacked boxes. At meal times, David or I donned our parkas, hats, and gloves and ventured into the frigid kitchen to heat up a can of chili or soup on the gas range. Being experienced backpackers, we might have enjoyed the adventure, had we not been shivering with fevers as well as from the cold.

I am grateful for electricity, but I cannot always rely on it. Nor do I trust my computer, so I save files on back-up disks. Through my own and others' experiences, I also have learned you cannot always depend on even the most dedicated doctors or nurses, or the latest medical diagnostic tests, surgeries, or treatments. People and their methods are fallible.

Even those closest to us may fail us in our greatest hour of need. Friends may turn away, unable to deal with their own pain or the awkwardness of facing ours. If you have been widowed, the couples with whom you and your spouse socialized may drop you from their invitation lists. Tragically, after the death of a child, many marriages dissolve. Thus, we may end up mourning not only the death of someone we love, but also the broken relationships with others whom we cherished and trusted.

Our relationship with God, however, is different. He never will abandon us, and His love never will fail. In our grief, God expresses His perfect love in His faithfulness, compassion, and presence, as well as in His gifts of strength, peace, hope, and joy. Throughout our lives, each of God's actions displays His love, because God is love. We see this most vividly expressed on the cross. "God demonstrates his own love for us in this: While we were still sinners, Christ died for us" (Romans 5:8).

In 1 Corinthians 13, the apostle Paul further defines this attribute of God as patient and kind. Friends who initially responded with gracious acts of kindness may tire of our sorrow and try to rush us through our grief. Yet God never runs out of lovingkindness as He accompanies us through the long, weary healing process. He also patiently helps us overcome our anger, doubts, and fears.

God expresses His unfailing love not only toward us, but also through us. As we yield to His Spirit, He enables us to respond to others with "love...patience, kindness" (Galatians 5:22). After Darren's death, many people compassionately expressed their sorrow, but a few twisted the sword that pierced my heart. In the power of God's Spirit, I could graciously respond and, if necessary, forgive. God also enabled my husband and I to lovingly work through the tensions that surfaced in our relationships and to support one another in our grief. We were drawn together by the power of His love rather than divided by the intensity of our pain. The Lord even supplied me with kindness and patience toward myself when I felt that my tears should have long since subsided.

When death strikes suddenly, unresolved conflicts with our loved ones may add to our hurt. Whatever the circumstances, we may feel abandoned by the one who has died. As we recognize and rely on God's love, we can forgive our loved ones and ourselves for any wrongs. We even can forgive others who we believe contributed to their death. God, who completely forgives us through Christ Jesus, longs to fill us with His perfect love, which "is not easily angered, it keeps no record of wrongs" (1 Corinthians 13:5).

As long as we live in this fallen world, we will experience pain and face disappointments. We will feel let down and we will let down others, because no human is completely reliable. But God is. We can confidently depend on the One who loves us completely and continually. "God is love," the apostle John assures us. And "love never fails" (1 Corinthians 13:8).

 Loving Father, help me to see and know Your love, which You graciously have displayed all around me. May I cling to Your unfailing love, which enables me to love You, myself, and others—even those who have hurt me. Thank You for Your constant and all-sufficient love. Amen.

Embracing God's Comfort

Read through 1 Corinthians 13:4-12, substituting "God" for "love." Which characteristic of God's love means the most to you right now? I encourage you to write down or talk to God about what that characteristic means to you.

_____

_____

_____

_____

_____

_____

Eternally Bound in Love

"For I am convinced that neither death nor life, neither angels nor demons, neither the present nor the future, nor any powers, neither height nor depth, nor anything else in all creation, will be able to separate us from the love of God that is in Christ Jesus our Lord." ~ Romans 8:38-39

"He's in a better place," well-meaning friends remind us. Or, if death followed a prolonged illness, they try to console us with, "At least she no longer suffers." Politely we nod our heads, but still our hearts break, because vital relationships have been severed. Death separated us from those we hold dear, and we have no hope of them returning to us during our life on earth.

Even though I held my son only eight months in my womb and four days in my arms, the mother-child bond was strong. While I never got to know him, I loved him and grieved his death deeply. If only he could return to me! I longed to care for him and to express my devotion to him, as well as to experience his love.

Years later, as I stood by my father's hospital bed, I again found it difficult to say good-bye. For fifteen years he had fought against death, and I knew it was now time for him to enter heaven. Still, sorrow filled my heart when my dad took his last breath.

In the midst of these times of grief, I found comfort in Romans 8:38-39. God promises us that such a separation never can occur in our relationship with Him. Nothing can sever us from His presence and love. In this world, job transfers can take away our friends, divorces can separate families, time steals our youthfulness, and death cuts our ties with those we cherish, but nothing, nothing, nothing can "separate us from the love of God that is in Christ Jesus our Lord."

The apostle Paul emphasizes this point with a series of antitheses. Neither death—ours or our loved ones'—nor life can separate us from God's love. Our anger toward God may blind us to His devotion, but it cannot erase it. Nor can haunting feelings of responsibility for another's death pry us from God's loving arms. God and His love remain steadfast in death and in life.

In trying to make sense of my son's death, I wondered if God allowed him to die because I loved my son too much. Perhaps Darren's life stood in the way of my relationship with God. Yet the Bible assures us that no one's life can separate us from His love. God certainly used my grief to draw me closer to the Lord and to show me the depths of His devotion, but He also has reminded me that all life is an expression of—not a barrier to—His love. Besides, God's love is much too big to be blocked by a 3 lb. 6 oz. baby.

The apostle Paul then assures us that neither angels nor demons can separate us from God's love. God's servants cannot, nor can Satan's accomplices. "The one who is in you is greater than the one who is in the world" (1 John 4:4). Certainly the powers of evil cannot overcome the force of God's powerful love.

The present cannot separate us, even though we may not feel His love at this moment. It is as real as our pain, as close as our tears. Nor can the future stand in the way of His devotion. We may fear the future and dread the lonely years ahead, yet God and His love go with us each day.

Neither height nor depth can separate us. As David the psalmist wrote, "Where can I go from your Spirit? Where can I flee from your presence? If I go up to the heavens, you are there; if I make my bed in the depths, you are there. If I rise on the wings of the dawn, if I settle on the far side of the sea, even there your hand will guide me, your right hand will hold me fast" (Psalm 139:7-10).

Lest he leave any loopholes, Paul assures us, "Nor anything else in all creation, will be able to separate us from the love of God that is in Christ Jesus our Lord." How could anything separate us from God's devotion once we are in Christ? When we trust in Jesus as our Savior, He takes up residence within us. We become one with God's perfect expression of His eternal love. Nothing we experience or do—good or bad—can subtract from, add to, or divide us from God's infinite love.

In the midst of our grief, we may lack "warm fuzzies" in our relationship with God. We may doubt His devotion, knowing that He permitted the death of one we cherish. But we find reassurance in remembering that our heavenly Father also allowed the death of His one and only Son, who cherishes us. Through Jesus' death and life, we're securely and eternally bonded to God and His unfailing love.

Father of unfailing love, I am thankful that nothing in this world nor the world to come can sever me from Your love once I am united with You through Christ Jesus. May I find my strength and security in Your great and eternal love. Amen.

Embracing God's Comfort

Does it feel like something has come between you and God's love? Talk to Him about it, and claim His promise that absolutely nothing can separate you from His love.

_____

_____

_____

_____

_____

_____

_____

_____

_____

_____

_____

Plumbing the Depth of God's Love

*"I pray that out of his glorious riches he may strengthen
you with power through his Spirit in your inner being,
so that Christ may dwell in your hearts through faith.
And I pray that you, being rooted and established in
love, may have power, together with all the saints, to
grasp how wide and long and high and deep is the
love of Christ, and to know this love that surpasses
knowledge—that you may be filled to the measure
of all the fullness of God." ~ Ephesians 3:16-19*

As my husband and I stood with our toes digging into the
warm Hawaiian sand, we were awestruck by the seemingly
endless ocean that stretched out before us. Then we donned
snorkels, masks, and fins to catch a glimpse of the wonders
concealed beneath its surface. I was impressed not only by
the incredible beauty of the coral and the variety of colorful
fish, but also by the reality that so much of our world remains
hidden from our sight. And while technological advancements
have enabled scientists to explore some of its mysteries, man
never will fathom the far reaches of the sea.

Even more shallow is our understanding of the infinite
depths of God's love. Paul, therefore, prays that his readers
will begin to grasp the devotion of their Savior, who gave His
life for them and now lives within them. I desire and pray
the same for you who have sought encouragement in these
pages.

I long for you to comprehend the width of God's love, which
encompasses every one of us and reaches into each area of
our lives. No wrong we have committed or loss we have
suffered can push us beyond the confines of His love. Even
in the dark lonely corner of our grief, His love resides with

us. Our friends may feel uncomfortable venturing into our world of sorrow, and even those closest to us may be unwilling or unable to offer comfort. We may feel that our grief has distanced us from everyone, yet we are never beyond God's reach. His outstretched arms span the width of this world and the breadth of even our most painful experiences.

I also join Paul in praying that you will grasp the length of Christ's love. He loved us long before we were created and will continue to love us throughout eternity. Though others leave us through death or desertion, God remains with us forever, expressing His endless love.

May you also see the height of our Savior's love. "For as high as the heavens are above the earth, so great is his love for those who fear him" (Psalm 103:11). As we kneel at His feet in awe, gazing up at our Lord, we realize that His love extends far past our field of vision. It has no ceiling, no limits.

Yet His love also extends far below us, into the depths of our despair. While I have felt close to God in worship services, as I've joined my voice with others in praising His name, my most intimate encounter occurred as I lay face down on the carpet, sobbing in grief. At that moment, the exalted Lord of all reached down and cradled me in His loving arms.

Whether you are rejoicing in God's greatness or desperately seeking solace in His nearness, may you grow in your knowledge of and trust in His love, which, as Paul writes, "surpasses knowledge." Just as we can never plunge the depths of the ocean, during our stay on earth we never will completely fathom the extent of God's immeasurable love. But each day we can grow in our understanding of His devotion as Christ dwells in our hearts through faith, and as we commune with Him through His Word.

We also can grow in our understanding as we take time to thank God for His expressions of love. Even in our darkest hours we can thank Him for His presence now and for His goodness throughout each year of our lives. And each day we can find and acknowledge at least one demonstration of His devotion.

In the midst of our grief, His love may seem hard to grasp, but we can pray Paul's prayer for ourselves, as well as for others who grieve alongside us. God Himself longs for us to know and to experience His love, and to believe that whether our hearts are filled with joy or seemingly broken beyond repair, He is with us. May we continually find strength in His presence and comfort in His embrace.

Loving Father, open my heart and mind that I might begin to comprehend the width, length, height, and depth of Your love. Thank You for sending Jesus to demonstrate this love through His life and His death, that I might experience Your grace and presence for all eternity. May Christ now dwell within me, strengthening me in this time of grief and forever filling me with Your love. Amen.

Embracing God's Comfort

Consider developing a plan for seeking God daily through His Word and prayer. When you feel a need for God's nearness, compassion, strength, hope, joy, faithfulness, or love, return to those sections in this book and meditate further on the verses. Continue to find your comfort in God's loving embrace.

_____

_____

_____

_____

_____

_____

_____

_____

_____

NOTES

14. Hope for the Hopeless

[1]Dee Brestin, "Falling in Love with Jesus," Women's Retreat at Grace Community Church, Auburn, Washington, May 2005.

20. Waiting for the Sunrise of Our Joy

[2]These descriptions of the stages and tasks of grieving are summarized from the following two books: Thomas Attig, *How We Grieve* (New York City: Oxford University Press, 1996), 42-43; and David Crenshaw, *Bereavement* (New York City: Continuum Publishing Co., 1990), 22-24.

22. Joy in God's Presence

[3]From "It Is Well With My Soul" by Horatio G. Spafford, 1873.

Suggestions for Group Use

We can find tremendous comfort in talking about our grief with others, especially with those who have suffered loss. Generally their own pain increases their understanding of ours. Thus, many experience mutual encouragement in support groups, as they walk the path of grief together.

Finding Comfort in God's Embrace can be an effective tool for grief support groups. I suggest using a nine-week format. At the first session, distribute the books and invite members to briefly share their story of loss. Then ask members to read one section each week, completing the applications.

During the initial meeting, emphasize the importance of confidentiality. What a person says in the group must stay in the group, unless that person has given permission to share it with others. This will help provide a safe environment for transparency. Also encourage group members to make the meetings a priority. Consistent attendance, as well as balanced sharing and listening, help create a strong support system.

With the group's permission, create a roster with names, addresses, phone numbers, and e-mail addresses. Copy and distribute it at the second meeting so that individuals can encourage each other during the week.

Using the "Embracing God's Comfort" sections, guide the group through your weekly sharing times. Read the suggested application from the first meditation for that week, then discuss the members' responses. When everyone has had an opportunity to share, move on to the next meditation's application. Members need not share from every journal entry, but encourage them to share at least once during your time together. Also, assure members that their sharing is not limited to their responses in "Embracing God's Comfort." These applications serve as a catalyst to your discussion, but if time allows, you also can ask questions such as, "What was most difficult for you this week? What was most encouraging?"

I suggest ending your group time with an opportunity to pray. You may wish to begin this time with one of the prayers from the section you have discussed. Then invite members to say brief one- or two-sentence prayers for themselves and one another. Close the prayer time with your own prayer or use another of the prayers from the book.

Support groups can meet in a home, Sunday school room, or other quiet and private space. Determine the start time and length of each meeting (ninety minutes works well), and commit to beginning and ending on schedule.

Your group can be as small as two and as large as twelve. To find individuals, announce the group through your church and other churches a few weeks before it starts. Hospital grief classes are another place to find interested people. Ask God to bring together the people who can best benefit from your group.

May God bless you as you help others find comfort in His embrace.

Finding Comfort in God's Embrace may be ordered through bookstores or directly from Main Street Book House. Quantity discounts are available. To order or for more information, contact us at:

www.mainstreetbookhouse.com

or write to:

Main Street Book House
P.O. Box 607
Auburn, WA 98071-0607